Postmodern
Theology

Postmodern Theology

Christian Faith
in a Pluralist World

Diogenes Allen
Robert N. Bellah
George A. Lindbeck
James B. Miller
Sandra M. Schneiders
Rowan D. Williams

Edited by

Frederic B. Burnham

HarperSanFrancisco
A Division of HarperCollins*Publishers*

Library of Congress Cataloging-in-Publication Data

Postmodern theology: Christian faith in a pluralist world / Diogenes Allen . . . [et al.]: edited by Frederic B. Burnham.—1st ed.
    p. cm.
    Includes bibliographies and index.
    ISBN   0-06-061231-2
    1. Theology—20th century—Congresses.   2. Postmodernism—
Congresses.   3. Religious pluralism—Christianity—Congresses.
I. Allen, Diogenes.   II. Burnham, Frederic B.   III. Trinity
Institute.
BR50.P63   1989
230—dc19   88-43268
                                                           CIP

91   92   93   MPC   10   9   8   7   6   5   4   3   2

Contents

Contributors

Diogenes Allen is Stuart Professor of Philosophy at Princeton Theological Seminary. He combines philosophy, theology, and spirituality in his work and is the author of several books in his field, among them *Philosophy for Understanding Theology.*

Robert N. Bellah is Ford Professor of Sociology and Comparative Studies at the University of California at Berkeley. The recently published bestseller *Habits of the Heart,* which he coauthored, is a study of American values, balanced in history and contemporary case study.

Frederic B. Burnham is the director of Trinity Institute, an agency of Trinity Church in New York City. A priest of the Episcopal church and a historian of science, he is the author and editor of a number of publications on the relationship between science and religion.

George A. Lindbeck is Pitkin Professor of Historical Theology at Yale University. His book *The Nature of Doctrine* is regarded as a landmark essay among theologians. In it he brings key contemporary philosophical issues to bear on the nature and formation of Christian doctrine.

James B. Miller serves as a chaplain to Carnegie-Mellon University and Chatham College. A graduate of the University of

Maryland and Union Theological Seminary in Virginia, Miller earned his Ph.D. in religious studies from Marquette University in Milwaukee. Also trained in mechanical engineering, Miller has had a long-standing interest in the relationship between theology and the sciences.

Sandra M. Schneiders, I.H.M., is associate professor of New Testament studies and spirituality at the Jesuit School of Theology at Berkeley. Trained in hermeneutical theology, she has published several essays in the field. Her recent contributions are an application of hermeneutics to feminist criticism.

Rowan D. Williams is Lady Margaret Professor of Divinity at Oxford University. His new voice on the Anglican theological scene raises doctrinal questions in the context of contemporary moral issues of justice and peace. His publications include *Resurrection* and *The Truce of God.*

Introduction

Frederic B. Burnham

The modern era in western civilization began with the scientific revolution in the seventeenth century. The discoveries of Copernicus, Kepler, Galileo, and Newton in astronomy and physics not only changed our picture of the cosmos, but also radically altered the way we think. A new conception of what knowledge is and how we come to know the truth about reality found expression in the philosophical systems of Bacon, Descartes, and Locke. No truths were taken for granted a priori. All valid knowledge was derived from the systematic investigation of experience. Any propositions not based upon empirical observation, propositions such as the existence of God and other tenets of faith, were banished to inferior epistemic status. Some philosophers even considered them meaningless.

As Robert Bellah argues in this volume, modern science offered "a new metalanguage," the language of facts, which it proclaimed to be *"really* true" and to which all the particular languages of culture and religion should be reduced. Before long everyone gave "unthinking priority to the world of scientific fact as the world of the really real." Even believers unconsciously accepted the second-class status of faith propositions and the language of the Bible. Banished from the province of reason and fact, theologians sought refuge in the language of feeling, a new but subjective foundation for belief. By the turn of the twentieth century, the scientific language of modernity had all but replaced the language of faith.

All this has now begun to change. Revelations in twentieth-century physics have totally undermined the epistemological pride of Victorian science and brought the modern era to a close. In the postmodern world of quantum phenomena, the foundation of reality itself is elusive and indeterminate. Scientific propositions about the essence of matter are at best enlightened approximations. As George Lindbeck observes in his chapter, it is now possible to hear exacting scholars "casually remark with the authority of the commonplace that the epistemological grounding of a physicist's quarks and a Homer's gods is exactly the same."

Furthermore, as Robert Bellah claims, it is generally recognized that scientific language can no longer be viewed as a set of universal, objective facts, "but rather as a set of research traditions" which, like religious language, is born out of a particular community of inquirers, "and unintelligible outside the lived practice of such communities." As George Lindbeck argues, all human experience is shaped, molded, and in a sense constituted by cultural and linguistic forms. Science is one of those cultural-linguistic systems; religion is another. Neither is necessarily nor epistemologically superior to the other. Human beings perceive the world through one or more of these communal languages.

The cultural hegemony of science has ended. The fundamental characteristic of the new postmodern era is epistemological relativism. A plurality of tongues now claims human allegiance. Though the language of the Bible is just one among many tongues, Christians no longer need be defensive. "In a postmodern world," as Diogenes Allen asserts, "Christianity is intellectually relevant."

The central question of this book, then, is, How do we tell the Christian story in a postmodern, pluralistic world? Certainly we must, as George Lindbeck maintains, restore the language of the Bible to its former currency in the culture, if possible. Beyond that, how do we address the postmodern world? How do we do postmodern theology? Each author provides an answer.

The offerings in this volume were written in response to Trinity Institute's invitation to a national conference held in New York and San Francisco in January 1987. Trinity Institute is a program for theological renewal supported by the Parish of Trinity Church in New York City. Its primary purpose is the stimulation of theological inquiry and the integration of that inquiry into the practice of ministry. Every year since 1968, the Institute has brought together renowned theologians and church leaders to explore issues of critical importance with clergy and laity of the Episcopal Church. In 1987, the speakers whose papers have been revised and edited for publication in this volume were asked to discuss the role of "The Church in a Postmodern Age."

The conference was occasioned in large measure by the publication of George Lindbeck's groundbreaking book, *The Nature of Doctrine: Religion and Theology in a Postliberal Age* (Westminster Press, 1984), which analyzes the state of contemporary theology and lays the foundation for a new cultural-linguistic approach to religion. In his book, Lindbeck, Pitkin Professor of Historical Theology at Yale University, criticizes the liberal agenda: the attempt of well-meaning theologians to translate the language of the Bible into the secular idiom in order to make the faith credible. In George Lindbeck's eyes, the Bible is a cultural-linguistic system which can only be distorted and diluted by translation. The Christian community's first and foremost responsibility in the cacophony of other postmodern tongues is simply to remain faithful to its native language, to preserve the integrity of the biblical tongue, even if that means shutting itself off temporarily from the secular culture. Lindbeck and some of his more conservative colleagues have been accused of ghettoism and fideism for suggesting that the rightful role of the contemporary church may be to withdraw from the world and pay attention solely to the purity of its own tongue. In his chapter, Lindbeck answers his critics by addressing the mission of the church to the culture at large. Each of the other authors tackles this issue as well, asking how the church can move beyond the mere preservation of its tongue to confront the world, without compromising the integrity of the kerygma.

In the opening essay, James B. Miller, a campus minister at Carnegie-Mellon University and former instructor at Marquette University, sets the conceptual scene for the volume. In a very careful and thorough manner, he analyzes the meaning of the terms "modern" and "postmodern" in both science and theology. His concluding remarks on postmodern theology are strikingly different from the positions of the rest of the authors, and more in the liberal tradition of dialogue with the sciences. Though his remarks are brief, they are suggestive of the new postmodern attempt at natural theology which can be found in the works of Arthur Peacocke, Robert Russell, and others not represented here.

The second essay, by Diogenes Allen, Stuart Professor of Philosophy at Princeton Theological Seminary, masterfully describes the collapse of "four pillars of modernity": self-sufficiency, reason, progress, and optimism. Professor Allen then demonstrates the failure of reason as a basis for moral discourse, and argues instead for the efficacy of the Christian premise, the "indefeasible value" of every human being, which is neither reasonable nor demonstrable but can be taken only on faith. Like Robert Bellah and Rowan Williams, Professor Allen is careful to confront the secular culture in the language of the Bible. He challenges the reigning secular concepts of personhood and justice through a close reading of the story of the Good Samaritan. Like George Lindbeck, he seeks to pull his reader into the "linguistic and imaginative world of the Bible."

The mission of the church to postmodern culture, according to George Lindbeck's essay, is to revive biblical literacy. For centuries, he argues, Western civilization was linguistically and imaginatively saturated with scripture, but the decline of biblical literacy in recent years has been "abrupt and pervasive," and public discourse has been drastically impoverished. No other language has replaced the biblical tongue in public life. Therefore, as Lindbeck suggests, "we have no common language in which to discuss the common weal." In fact, "society as a whole, and to a large extent the church also, has become a communicative basket-case."

The postmodern climate, Lindbeck claims, is open to the "textualization of reality," the close reading of classical texts like the Bible "in order to see what the world looks like in and through them." The Bible could make a comeback! But Lindbeck is not wholly optimistic about that prospect. First, he is not convinced that the churches are up to it, because within the churches biblical literacy is still in decline. Second, history has taught us that the Christianization of culture is not always a good thing. The church must not confuse "the biblical shaping of the social mind and imagination" with the actual exercise of social power.

In his essay, Lindbeck acknowledges the cultural fruits of reviving the biblical language, and to that extent answers his critics. Relearning the language of Zion is still imperative for its own sake, but Lindbeck now numbers himself among those who would "relearn that language not simply in order to better sing God's praises, but also out of concern for the societies in which we live."

Sandra Schneiders, like Diogenes Allen and George Lindbeck, is not convinced that the church is ready or able to take advantage of its postmodern opportunities. Not only has the church itself been largely responsible for the eclipse of biblical literacy, but it is now just one voice among many, and fast becoming a minority position in our pluralistic culture. Professor Schneiders, who teaches at the Jesuit School of Theology in Berkeley, has reason to be both encouraged and discouraged about the postmodern message of the Bible. Like Hans Frei and George Lindbeck, she sees hope in the new postcritical hermeneutical approach to the Bible. "Scholars," she writes, "are coming to realize that the locus of revelation for the contemporary Christian is not the events behind the texts, nor the theology of the biblical authors, nor even the preaching of the texts in the community, but the texts themselves as language that involves the reader." Thus the modern objectification of the biblical text has given way to a postmodern "hermeneutical paradigm of understanding by participative dialogue." We have learned a great deal about scripture through the critical eye of modernity, but now the door to a "deeper and richer encounter" with the text has been opened.

Nevertheless, Schneiders finds patriarchy to be so deeply ingrained in the text as to obscure the Bible's message. She reviews feminist attempts to excise patriarchy from the text and argues that the results are inconclusive. "Unless the church as a whole takes this entire issue much more seriously," she warns, "I and others like me may be forced to conclude that the Bible does not have a life-giving message for the postmodern world."

Robert Bellah, Ford Professor of Sociology and Comparative Studies at the University of California at Berkeley, also considers the fundamental difference between modern and postmodern times to be linguistic. In the modern era, scientific method split the linguistic world in two. On the one hand, there was the objective language of scientific fact to which the culture gave unthinking priority. On the other hand, there was the necessary but secondary language of feeling. In *Habits of the Heart,* Bellah and his coauthors called the languages of fact and feeling "utilitarian and expressive individualism" and suggested that "the combination of these two ways of speaking is our first language, our dominant view of reality in American culture." Contemporary scholars and philosophers, however, no longer accept the linguistic hegemony of science and, as all our authors agree, the door is open again for the language of the Bible.

Bellah, however, takes the linguistic analysis one step beyond Lindbeck. We live, he maintains, in a linguistic world which, in the absence of a scientific metalanguage, is genuinely pluralistic. We Christians not only should relearn our language, we must also become genuinely multilingual, speaking each cultural language in its appropriate context. In this manner, Bellah proposes to escape the charge of parochialism which has been levied against Lindbeck.

When Bellah turns to the language of the Bible itself, he puts Lindbeck's linguistic theories into practice. The words of the beatitudes, he argues, "create a world just as surely as the word of God in Genesis 1 creates the heavens and the earth and all that is in them." He demonstrates convincingly just how the Beatitudes create the world of the heavenly kingdom. Furthermore, he illustrates, as an operational principle, how that world of the heavenly kingdom can be used to confront the world of contemporary culture. He practices not apologetic, but proactive encounter with the world.

Rowan Williams, Lady Margaret Professor of Divinity at Oxford University, devotes his whole essay to this same mission. It is not enough, he concurs, simply to learn anew the language of Zion. We are called also to a creative encounter with culture. The language of the Bible, he argues, is the language of parables. Often Jesus simply tells a story. Those stories confront the hearer and make personal transformation possible. In the same manner, the church should confront and transform the world. "Theology," Williams concludes, should "equip us to speak and act parabolically as Christians, to construct in our imaging and our acting 'texts' about conversion—not translations of doctrine into digestible forms, but effective images of a new world."

Like Bellah and Allen, Williams puts the cultural-linguistic concepts of Lindbeck into practice. In fact, all three of them, in their exegesis of biblical stories, demonstrate effectively how postmodern theology ought to be practiced. In that all-important respect, this book has the advantage of practicing what it preaches.

Postmodern
Theology

1. The Emerging Postmodern World

James B. Miller

Most observers of contemporary history acknowledge that western civilization is undergoing a fundamental shift in world-view. In addition, it is generally agreed that this shift has been spurred on by the discoveries and theoretical developments which have occurred in the natural sciences over the past 150 or so years. This is an ongoing shift, and the detailed character of the emerging worldview is still somewhat hazy. Nevertheless, its general features do appear fairly clear.

The following is an attempt to outline those features. The new perspective they constitute could be called many things, but here it will be identified as postmodern. As this label implies, the chief elements of the emerging worldview may be seen in sharpest contrast against the immediately preceding perspective, namely the modern one. Further, a full appreciation of the currently developing worldview requires a consideration of the premodern culture from which modernism sprang.

A thorough treatment of the premodern world is not within the scope of this essay. Nevertheless, the following aspects of that culture should be taken into account.

The premodern world was formed through the convergence of Greek speculative cosmological ideas and an essentially Hebraic theological cosmology. By the time of the appearance of the Christian church, the philosophies of Plato and Aristotle had come to dominate Greek thought. Following the fall of the Roman Empire and the cultural fragmentation which occurred in its aftermath, there was a recovery of classical Greek thought in the Christian West in the eleventh and twelfth centuries. Beyond simple recovery, there was the forging of a firm bond between Aristotelian philosophy (natural and otherwise) and Christian theology. Chief among those making this synthesis possible was Thomas Aquinas.

The main elements of this premodern worldview were the following: a vertical metaphysical dualism, separating the celestial from the terrestrial spheres; a language of purpose (primarily organic metaphors) to describe the things in, and the order of, the cosmos; a reliance upon tradition as a source of authoritative knowledge; a view of humanity as standing at the center of the cosmos.

By the eve of the birth of modern culture, the relation between Aristotelian science (including a geocentric cosmological model developed by the second-century astronomer Ptolemy) and Christian theology had become so integral that it was virtually impossible to determine where one stopped and the other began. As a consequence, it was difficult to see how a philosophical or cosmological challenge to the system of Aristotelian natural philosophy could be anything less than a challenge to theological orthodoxy as well. Thus, the stage was set for the Copernican-Galilean controversy out of which modern culture emerged and in which natural science as a discipline became independent of the intellectual or theological authority of the Christian church.

THE MODERN WORLD

Although the rise of modern culture is often described as a triumph of critical rationality over religious dogmatism, it began in fact as an essentially philosophical controversy, namely, one between the prevailing Aristotelianism and a recovered Pythagorean Platonism. Further, the condemnation, recantation, and final house imprisonment of Galileo in the seventeenth century must be understood more as a product of the broader social struggle over authority (political and religious) generated by the Protestant Reformation than as a consequence of a conflict between natural science and theology.

Be that as it may, the shift in worldview begun by Copernicus and Galileo, a shift from organic models emphasizing final causality to mathematical and geometric models emphasizing efficient (or mechanical) causality, helped initiate an era in which the cosmic holism of the premodern period was torn apart.

Two scientist-philosophers were especially significant in the formation of the modern worldview: René Descartes and Immanuel Kant. Descartes, in fact, is often identified as the father of the modern era. For Descartes, the cosmos was divided into two radically different substantial domains: that of matter and that of mind (or spirit). The sciences proper were concerned with the former and developed rational mathematical and mechanical models to account for behavior of entities in the material domain. The domain of mind or spirit was fundamentally different from that of matter. It was the domain in which divine revelation and theological authority prevailed. As a result of this division, what might be called a horizontal dualism became firmly established in the Western cultural psyche.

Although Descartes's specific proposals for a mechanistic physics were largely superseded by Newton's later mathematical system, the *dualism* which Descartes initiated with his earliest cosmological speculations, and which sustained his view of the material world as a vast machine, prevailed. Efficient or mechanical causality came to be the sufficient explanatory category for the material world.

The second defining characteristic of the modern era was the rise of "critical" thought. Immanuel Kant is usually cited as the progenitor of critical rationality. Kant was especially concerned with epistemological questions; that is, questions dealing with what knowledge is and how we know what we know.

In the past, the question which had been asked was how the mind (an immaterial entity) conformed itself to objects in the world (material entities). Kant proposed that this question be turned around; that is, he began by asking not how the mind conformed itself to the world but instead how the world conformed itself to the mind.

In a manner similar to that of Descartes, who had divided the cosmos into material and mental (or spiritual) substances, Kant divided the realm of knowledge into two fundamentally separate domains: that of the phenomena and that of the noumena. For Kant, empirical knowledge was not a direct mirror of the world, but rather a product of the interaction of the senses with the ordering activity of the mind. Phenomena were the products of this interaction. Knowledge in the proper sense was limited by Kant to knowledge of phenomena.

But what of the noumena? These were of two sorts: either things in themselves (i.e., the world apart from the constructive activity of human intellect), or those objects of which, in principle, no sensory experience was possible, for example, the universe as a causal whole, the human self as a free agent, and God. For Kant there could be no proper knowledge of these noumenal entities.

Yet, in order for there to be science at all, it was necessary to believe that the world was a causal whole. In order for human activity to be held accountable to moral standards, it was necessary to assume the existence of a freely acting self. In order for the world to be more than a mere aggregate of disparate objects and causal chains, it was necessary to affirm a perfect unifying principle for all existence; namely, God. Therefore, though *knowledge* of the world as a whole, of the self, and of God were denied by Kant, *faith* in them, he argued, was absolutely necessary for practical reasons. Thus, as Descartes had divided the cosmos into the realms of matter and of mind, in a parallel fashion Kant divided it into the realms of pure and practical reason, of knowledge and faith, of empirical understanding and ethics, of the scientific and the religious.

This comprehensive dualism has been the central mark of modern culture. It has come to be manifest in a variety of forms, sometimes very ironically. For example, the logical positivist movement implicitly accepted this dualism, but then denied meaningfulness to the nonempirical, nonscientific side (i.e., the domain of the noumenal). Reductionists sought to explain religion and religious phenomena in exclusively scientific (or social scientific) terms, thus denying the autonomy (or independent reality) of the religious (i.e., explaining the noumenal in terms of the phenomenal). In contrast, the existentialist movement, while also implicitly accepting the dualism, invested all significant meaning on the side of faith, moral action, and the religious life (i.e., in the noumenal domain).

THEOLOGY IN THE MODERN AGE

There were a variety of theological responses to this broad cultural shift, some of which I shall mention briefly.

Friedrich Schleiermacher, regarded by some as the father of modern Protestantism, was a German theologian deeply influenced by the philosophy of Kant. He was one of the first to see the theological implications of modern, critical philosophy. Doubt about the capacity to know God through rational inquiry into nature, and suspicion about the worth of metaphysical speculation, left theology in desperate need of new ground for its claims.

Schleiermacher articulated such a new ground for theology. In the interior life of the self, claimed Schleiermacher, there is a religious sense akin to the aesthetic sphere, and as universal to humanity as rational and moral consciousness. He claimed that all persons had, on occasion, an immediate sense of absolute dependence, and this is the ground for reference to God. Since this new foundation for religious consciousness was regarded as no less intrinsic to human selfhood than the moral and rational aspects of consciousness, one could presume ultimate continuity between religious faith and the light of reason as expressed. Christian faith and scientific inquiry were thus taken to be compatible, but separate, domains of human experience.

Liberal Protestant theologians following after Schleiermacher, such as Albrecht Ritschl, Adolf von Harnack, and others, emphasized the continuity of God with man, of religion with culture. They tended to link salvation closely with ethical progress in history—the domain of rational, free, and moral personhood, and the domain which expressed human supremacy over nature. Much as Schleiermacher had done, liberal Protestants turned their attention to the religious subject. Natural theology was virtually abandoned.

Karl Barth, perhaps the most important neo-Reformation theologian to emerge in this century, was a student of liberalism but began a decisive turn away from it early in his career. Barth rejected the close identity between Christianity and culture, emphasizing instead a dialectical relation between the "Word of God" and the "word of man." But quite significantly, his break with liberalism was not a clean break from the modern worldview. Both neo-Reformation theologians such as Barth, and neo-Thomist theologians such as Karl Rahner, had been deeply influenced by existentialism. As mentioned above, the existentialists had relinquished the natural world to the sciences and placed paramount interest in the human person—the realm of freedom and value, transcending natural processes. Thus, focus on the human subject as the locus of God's self-disclosure continued in these forms of twentieth-century theology.

It is important to note that some neoorthodox theologies have also manifested a kind of positivism. One finds in them an uncritical confidence that the revelatory "word" (either in scripture or in tradition) provides a kind of absolute knowledge of God and God's purpose for the world. This confidence is parallel to that found among the logical positivists, who held that reason and empirical observation were the sole and sufficient sources of absolute knowledge of the world.

Thus, one can reasonably claim that the modern worldview continues to form the dominant perspective in contemporary Western and Christian culture. It is found in the popular understanding of science as an impersonal, detached, and objective search for the facts of nature. Its neoorthodox theological manifestation is "normal" Christian theology. The prophetic rhetoric of this theology justifies a program of cultural change through social action. Its existentialist roots encourage contemporary forms of pastoral care and spiritual renewal which turn people away from their intrinsic relation to nature and history and focus them on a kind of atemporal personhood. It offers a revealed (and so, absolute) dogmatics of transcendence for those who would claim for Christianity a right to cultural dominance.

Yet the hegemony of this philosophical and related theological tradition is on the wane. This decline is due, first, to developments which have occurred within the sciences themselves and, second, to philosophical developments growing out of reflection on that scientific activity. The postmodern era may be far from midday, but it is well past dawn.

THE POSTMODERN WORLD

Developments in biology and in physics have been contributing to the emergence of a fundamentally new worldview. The prevailing images for the premodern world were organic. Those for the modern world were mechanical and dualistic. The characteristic images for the postmodern world are historical, relational, and personal.

First, the world is *evolutionary*. It is not simply here. The world is understood today to be developing by means of environmental selection among indeterminate variations of form. In previous eras an entity was understood to be what it was because it embodied an eternal essence, and that essence determined its nature and value. In the radically contingent and historical world of contemporary biology, one in which what an entity may become cannot be known beforehand, the idea of a determining essence has become seriously problematic.

The world is not so much a creation as a *creating*. And human beings are both a product of and, for now, participants in this ongoing creating. Humanity is understood to be a contingent (i.e., not necessary) product of universal natural processes, rather than the crowning act of creation whereby a particular eternal essence was made actual through specific divine commands. Further, that creative dynamic is seen as ongoing.

Second, the world is understood to be relative, indeterminate, and participatory. Existence is fully relative; that is, nothing exists in and of itself. To be is to be *related*. In a Newtonian world it was possible to conceive of absolute contexts of space and time within which an object could be isolated. But with Einstein's development of relativity physics, common-sense notions of the absoluteness of space and time have been abandoned. It can no longer be taken for granted that measurements of either distance or duration in one frame of reference will be identical to those taken in another. In fact, the motion of the reference frame determines the measure.

Further, with the advent of quantum theory, the common-sense notion of a substantial universe in any sense (i.e., a universe comprised of self-sufficient things) has become highly suspect. At its most fundamental level, the universe does not seem to be composed of stuff or things at all but rather of dynamic relations. Or, to say it another way, the world is not a thing which has a history; it *is* history.

As quantum theory has developed, it has become evident that certain characteristics are coupled in such a way that to determine one characteristic is to disable one from determining the other. Werner Heisenberg expressed this finding in his principle of uncertainty. It seems that at the core of reality there is an uncertainty (or indeterminacy) which no amount or quality of observation can overcome. This conclusion runs sharply counter to the modern presupposition that the world is open, in principle, to full and complete description. It suggests that at the core of reality is an unfathomable *mystery.*

But this also means that the future cannot be fully determined either. This is not because there is insufficient data from which to make a determinate prediction, but rather because the processes of the world itself have only probable results; that is, *you cannot be absolutely certain what the outcome will be beforehand.*

A final consequence of the development of quantum physics has to do with the issue of objectivity. From the modern perspective, the sciences deal with objective knowledge which derives from detached, impersonal observation of the facts of nature. Contemporary physics, however, has effectively shown that, while there can be a relative objectivity in the practice of science (i.e., one due to the adherence of the individual scientist to a set of procedures accepted by the community), there is no observation in which the object observed and the subject observing are absolutely separate. That is to say, there are no "facts" in nature independent of some particular observer. In the process of knowing the world, there are no more spectators. *All knowers are participants in that which is to be known.*

In summary, the development of evolutionary theory in biology and of relativity and quantum theories in physics has led to a vision of the world, not as a thing which has a history, but as history itself. The world has come to be seen not as a system of independent atomic parts linked together by external mechanical relations but, instead, as a dynamic nexus of internal relatings, actual and potential.

WHAT DOES IT MEAN "TO KNOW"?

This broad shift in worldview has had incorporated within it a shift in the understanding of what knowledge is, and how it is that we know. In philosophical terms, these shifts have been in the field of epistemology. Here again, the themes of evolution, relativity, indeterminacy, and participation have appeared.

In the postmodern context, all knowledge is viewed as cultural artifact. For example, Ludwig Wittgenstein has argued that language is best understood not in terms of a formal logic, but rather as a form of human activity (a game), which is instrumental to a set of human purposes (a form of life). The significance of a particular language game (e.g., science) is not that it somehow captures in explicit expression something of the nature of reality, but instead that it serves to support the achievement of certain ends. This contextual understanding of the character of language sharply undercuts any form of positivism (scientific, philosophical, theological), because positivisms assume that language can have absolute or noncontextual meaning.[1] From a postmodern perspective, all knowledge is historically implicated. Nothing is known apart from its cultural setting, and that setting is constitutive of what is known. There are no culturally neutral facts. *Knowledge is not so much found as made, or better, it does not grow so much as it is grown.*

Today this biological analogy seems especially apt, and from a postmodern perspective, the processes by which knowledge arises are perhaps best characterized as evolutionary and ecological. Karl Popper, Thomas Kuhn, and Stephen Toulmin have been especially helpful in showing how knowledge does not accumulate in a simple additive fashion. Popper has shown how science is not simply a rational enterprise but ultimately depends upon a nonlogical exercise of the creative human imagination. Kuhn pioneered the analysis of science as a dynamic historical phenomenon, in which fundamental shifts in theory are not simply logical modifications or reinterpretations of past knowledge, but are instead radical transformations of worldview.

In yet another view, different from both of these positions, Toulmin has argued persuasively that human knowing should be understood as an ecological process paralleling in the epistemological domain what is found in the biological. Knowledge, for Toulmin, exhibits both a transformative dynamism in which older ideas are continuous with newer ones, and a rationality grounded in intentionality rather than logicality. Thus, the process of inquiry not only adds new "facts" but transforms (and at times discards) old ones. As new concepts emerge, other concepts adapt and some concepts become extinct. There is a nonlogical relationship between the older systems of knowledge and the new systems by which they are replaced. The pursuit of knowledge always involves human (individual and corporate) purposes and goals.

Michael Polanyi also began with reflections on scientific practice. However, his contribution to the emerging postmodern perspective has been to show that the modern distinction between objective and subjective knowing is illusory and that all knowing is personal; that is, dependent upon the commitment of the knower within a community of value.

A word should be said here about the concept of truth. From the postmodern perspective, truth is no longer a term of measurement, indicating a form of correspondence between our ideas and the substance of the real. Instead, truth is a functional and a valuational term. Polanyi argues that the claim of truthfulness indicates our participation in an intersubjective community committed to knowing that reality which is immanent within, yet transcendent of, any individual or community of knowers.

Because truth is relative to the community of knowers, all knowledge is incomplete. More can always be said. Such incompleteness is made evident not only in further positive statements of what is known but also in the anomalies (i.e., inconsistencies, incoherencies) found within what is said to be known.

Earlier in this chapter, I noted that developments in the sciences, both physical and biological, were suggesting that the world was best viewed not as a thing with a history, but as history. Alfred North Whitehead is the twentieth-century philosopher who, informed by postmodern science, has most comprehensively described such a worldview. Whitehead described the world not in terms of substances (things) but in terms of events (temporal units of relatedness). Here is a vision of the world in which dynamic temporality rather than static substantiality is the central factor in all existence. Whitehead's thought, which included an explicitly theological element, has stimulated a variety of efforts in the Christian community, both Protestant and Roman Catholic, to reconsider the affirmations of the Christian heritage in relation to a contemporary understanding of the world as a whole.

These then are the general features of the postmodern perspective. It is worth the effort to consider how a shift to this worldview might affect the ways in which the Christian community has affirmed its faith. In that regard, the following comments are offered on the doctrine of creation, the doctrine of "man," and together the doctrines of the incarnation and the *eschaton*.

THE TENSE OF CREATION

Throughout the Christian community it is common to hear God referred to as creator in the past tense. There is ordinarily a distinction made between God's creation of the cosmos at some point in the past and God's providential sustaining of the cosmos which God created. However, it is difficult to know the significance of this past tense, given a world which is not finished, a world which is evolving. The world has not so much been created as it is being created.

It does not help to point to the "Big Bang" as though this particular model for the origin of the world provided some sort of empirical verification of a doctrine of *creatio ex nihilo*. Quite the contrary, if this model is sustained as the preferred one, and even if in principle science is never able to get empirically before the "Big Bang," one need not conclude that there was some primordial moment before which there was nothing. There is a sense in which this way of talking theologically continues to assume both a dualistic relationship between God and the world and also the notion of the world as a thing. In the postmodern setting neither of these assumptions seems adequate or appropriate.

The language about God as creator needs to be more self-consciously transitive. God did not simply create the world in the past, God has been creating the world as far back as we can know and is creating the world yet today. Again, looking toward an open future, it is unclear what it would mean to say that God's creating was finished.

In addition, while God may be the most original, the most comprehensive, the most significant participant in the creating, God is not the only creating agent. Unless one is prepared to accept some form of historical determinism, every element of the world participates not only in its own creation but in the creation of the universe as a whole. We are what we are because of what quarks did and what quarks do, but we are also what we are, and will become what we will be, because of what we do. Again, to adopt a theological language in which God is the only authentic creator requires both a cosmological dualism and an historical determinism.

THE DOCTRINE OF "MAN"

Just as language which separates God from the world seems inappropriate in the postmodern setting, so also is theological language which would separate humanity from the world. The prevailing theological anthropology in the Church tends to take the human focus of the Genesis account of creation for granted. Even among those for whom an evolutionary account of the emergence of life is acceptable, there remains an implicit judgment that human beings are qualitatively distinct from the rest of the world, living and nonliving. This distinction lies at the heart of all appraisals which would see humanity at the center of the universe, and which would understand human history to be either distinct from or at the point of the arrow of universal history.

Such examples of species pride are commonplace in the pulpit rhetoric of the Church, yet they appear inappropriate in at least two respects. First, the emergence of humankind as a distinct species in the history of life is distinctive only in the same sense that all historical events are distinct and unique. The processes out of which human beings emerged are not different, in principle, from those out of which all else in the universe arose, whether animal, vegetable, or mineral.

Secondly, the human-centeredness of much of Christian theology (though understandable in the sense that if trees have theology, then trees probably occupy the central place in it) seems inappropriate in the face of the likelihood that there will be no human beings 100,000 years from now. In cosmic time, this is but a blink of the eye. Yet in terms of the history of homo sapiens, this just about covers the route.

There are at least two grounds on which one can feel confident about claiming that homo sapiens will disappear. The first has to do with the immediate prospect for survival of the species. There are many today who doubt that a thermonuclear holocaust can be avoided. Such a disaster, such a mass extinction, would be especially poignant in the history of life on this planet since most extinctions have not been self-induced.

But one need not take this pessimistic view in order to judge that human beings will have a brief (on a cosmic time scale) tenure. The process of evolution did not stop with the appearance of the first Cro-Magnon. Should present humanity survive long enough to begin to populate nearby space, the new environments will bring with them selective pressures that will have the potential for radically transforming human physiognomy. And this says nothing of the power to increase the rate of evolutionary change that human culture is already making possible through the biological sciences. The point is that we may well wonder whether Zinjanthropus or even Neanderthal were "human"; but it is also appropriate to look forward into the mists of the future and wonder whether the "Star Child" will be "human."

Perhaps even closer at hand is the question of where developments in the fields of computer and cognitive sciences will lead. If HAL-9000 (the artificial intelligence in Arthur C. Clarke's *2001: A Space Odyssey*) is not human, what is the appropriate species designation? Will not artificially intelligent systems be our "offspring"? In this context I must even wonder what the qualifier "artificial" really means.

One additional comment on the human focus of Christian theology. If it is uncertain what one is referring to when Adam is spoken of in historical terms, then it is even more unclear what is meant when "The Fall" is spoken of as though it were an historical event. If we are to speak in an illuminating way about evil in the universe, or, more particularly, about pervasive evil in human experience, then we need new stories which account for the reality of our experience of sin, stories which do not assume that the contemporary experience of evil is in some way a mechanical consequence of the act of a prehistoric ancestor.

INCARNATION AND ESCHATOLOGY: THE NTH COMING OF THE CHRIST

In an evolutionary, relativistic, and indeterminate world, one in which human beings (as well as to one degree or another all elements of the cosmos) are seen as both creatures and cocreators of the world and of truth, it seems peculiar to understand the doctrine of the incarnation as referring to only one particular moment in cosmic history. Traditionally, incarnation has been the doctrinal symbol of the union of God as transcendent and immanent, of God as the One whose primordial word is made flesh in an historical moment. But is this moment singular? Does incarnation refer only to Jesus of Nazareth? Or does incarnation to one extent or another characterize every moment in the history of the universe?

To be sure, for the Christian tradition, Jesus of Nazareth is both the one who articulates the incarnational model in his teaching and the one who in his person is said to demonstrate the meaning of that model for human living. In this sense Jesus' uniqueness as incarnation is historical but not ontological (e.g., scripture itself speaks of Jesus as the first fruits, the first of many). From a postmodern perspective, the dynamics of incarnation might be thought of in John Cobb's terms. God speaks the divine word, the logos, the divine intention for a particular moment of human history; the logos is fully actualized, fully enfleshed in the acts forming the particular human life of Jesus of Nazareth; since Jesus is affirmed paradigmatically as the one in whom the word is made flesh, he is affirmed as the Christ; yet, to the extent that any human person makes concrete (actualizes) the intention of God for that life, then to that extent Christ is manifest in that life (or as Paul put it, "It is not I who live but Christ who lives in me").

Finally, from a postmodern perspective the doctrine of incarnation also appears to bear within itself both eschatology and apocalypse: that is, the last days are always here and now and the emergent reality (the future) is always fundamentally new. Therefore, we may come to appreciate the integration of incarnation, eschatology and apocalypse in a new way for our age.

These, then, are a few observations about how the emerging postmodern worldview might have an impact on the received Christian theological tradition. Beyond doctrine, the worldview will also have an impact on how ministry is conceived, but the exploration of these implications would be the topic of yet another essay.

To close, perhaps it is sufficient to say that we in the Christian community stand in the midst of a time of fundamental cultural transition. Faithfulness in such a time depends on our ability to discern and join with the movement of that spirit which is making all things new. We, like Abraham of old, are called upon to sojourn in a strange land and there to build altars in word and deed, glorifying the one who is lovingly bringing this new world into being.

NOTE

1. George Lindbeck's analysis of Theology in his recent book, *The Nature of Doctrine: Religion and Theology in a Postliberal Age* (Philadelphia: Westminster Press, 1984), draws heavily upon Wittgenstein's Theory of Language games.

2. Christian Values in a Post-Christian Context

Diogenes Allen

Ludwig Wittgenstein, considered to be one of the greatest philosophers of the twentieth century, confided in one of his notebooks that

A culture is like a big organization which assigns each of its members a place where he can work in the spirit of the whole; and it is perfectly fair for his power to be measured by the contribution he succeeds in making to the whole enterprise. In an age without culture on the other hand forces become fragmented and the power of an individual man is used up in overcoming opposing forces and frictional resistances; it does not show in the distance he travels but perhaps only in the heat he generates in overcoming friction. But energy is still energy and even if the spectacle which our age affords us is not the formation of a great cultural work, with the best men contributing to the same great end, so much as the unimpressive spectacle of a crowd whose best members work for purely private ends, still we must not forget that the spectacle is not what matters.

I realize then that the disappearance of a culture does not signify the disappearance of human value, but simply of certain means of expressing this value, yet the fact remains that I have no sympathy for the current of European civilization and do not understand its goals, if it has any.[1]

This is a description of alienation. Wittgenstein, like so many others in our century, could not find a public life to which he could make a positive contribution. His lament is a noble one, but I think that we today are increasingly in a situation in which we can do more than lament, because the modern world which, generally speaking, has become so alien to Christianity is beginning to pass away. We are used to the idea that we live in a post-Christian age, but we are actually entering a postmodern one. What is crumbling are the pillars of western society, which were erected during the Enlightenment.

There are at least four areas in which this breakdown is evident. The most fundamental is that it can no longer be claimed as a commonly accepted philosophical and scientific tenet that we live in a self-contained universe. That widely held conviction has dominated the intellectual world of the university and research centers. It developed gradually from an interpretation of the natural world provided by the rise of modern science in the seventeenth century. The possible reality of God could be ignored without any consequences at all for our understanding of the natural world and history. To believe in God was permissible as a private opinion, but the question of whether there is a God was not important nor even an inescapable issue for inquiring minds.

The philosophical and scientific bases for excluding the possibility of God have collapsed. It is not meaningless, after all, to ask, Why does the universe exist, this particular one or, for that matter, any universe at all? Hume's and Kant's quite sophisticated objections have been found to fail. This was first shown in 1970, by William L. Rowe, a nonbeliever, writing in the analytic school of philosophy.[2] The conviction that we live in a self-contained universe can no longer be supported by a philosophic consensus. The order and existence of the natural world, although they do not of themselves establish the existence of God, nonetheless legitimately lead us to ask: Is nature's existence and order the result of an external cause?

This development in philosophy has been reinforced by developments in cosmology. According to the Big Bang theory of the origin of our present cosmos, our universe was once a very dense, tiny mass that then exploded and is still expanding. That initial dense mass had very specific properties. Its specific nature leads us to ask, Why do we have this specific mass, from which our present order has arisen, rather than another? This specificity is even more remarkable because life could not have arisen in our universe if the properties of this mass had been only slightly different. The question of why we have this universe rather than another arises within science itself for the first time in scientific history. (The questions cannot be answered from a study of the relations between the members of our universe. The only possible way to answer the question with science is to go outside our universe and posit *other* universes with which we now have no contact.)

These developments in philosophy and science only show us the *possibility* of God. But the possibility is raised by developments in the very domains which earlier had been used to close off the possibility. We have had quite a *volte face*.

Once the embargo on the possibility of God is lifted, it is easy to show that the issue of divine existence is intellectually inescapable. For example, human beings are goal-seeking. Our goals are numerous and in some instances conflicting. To be rational, we must order them into some priority. This is true of us as individuals and as members of various social and political groups.

To order our goals rationally, we must make a match between our needs, interests, and desires, on the one hand, and what the physical and social environments permit us reasonably to hope we can achieve, on the other hand. Our estimate is greatly affected by whether we think this universe is ultimate or not. An estimate based on the conviction that the universe is ultimate is significantly different from an estimate based on the view that it is not. So the need to direct and order our lives as individuals and as societies is a reason to pursue the question of the status of our universe. Our goal-seeking behavior renders the question of the status of the universe *inescapable* for rational agents.

In addition to being goal-seeking, we have needs, aspirations, and desires that are far greater than can be satisfied should this universe be all that there is. If the universe is ultimate, then we must greatly *reduce* our aspirations, and suffer the frustration of many of our needs and desires. To assume that we must pay this price is rational and sensible only if we have examined the status of the universe, and indeed examined it seriously and carefully.

All people are now in the position in which it is sensible to become a seeker. If people are sensible, they will earnestly want to know whether this universe is ultimate or not. There is therefore no need for Christians to continue to be defensive. Just as Socrates did in ancient Greece, we have a mission: to challenge the supposition that the status of the universe and our place in it have already been settled by science and philosophy. On strictly intellectual grounds, scientific and philosophic, we do not know. Both individuals and institutions ought to consider and study anything which promises to shed light on our situation. We have the opportunity and the task of turning people into seekers, as did Socrates, with confidence that if one seeks, one is likely to find.

The second breakdown of the modern world is the failure to find a basis for morality and society. A major project of the

Enlightenment was to base traditional morality and society on reason rather than on religion. It sought to show by reason alone that some things are wrong in nearly all circumstances, that to become a moral person is of supreme importance for the individual and for society, and that moral behavior is objective and not a matter of individual choice, nor relative to a society. The deepest of all our traditional moral convictions is that every person has intrinsic value. But it is now argued that all attempts to give morality and society a secular basis are bankrupt.[3]

When as individuals and as a society we chose the traditional morality defined above, heavily influenced by some of the best views of ancient Greek culture and Christianity, the failure of secular philosophy did not matter for practical purposes. But today traditional morality is being discarded, and we find ourselves in the time of the Judges, in which each does what is right in his or her own sight.

The third pillar of the Enlightenment is belief in inevitable progress. Modern science and technology so improved life that they led to a belief in progress, and in time to belief in *inevitable* progress. We are now faced with our failure to eradicate such serious social and economic problems as crime, pollution, poverty, racism, and war, and we are becoming uneasy. We may be able to surmount our difficulties, but it is not *inevitable* that we shall. The optimism of inevitable progress has become tarnished. Part of the optimism of the modern period was founded on a belief in the power of education and science to free us from social bondage and from nature's bondage. But there is an increasing concern that education and social reform may not be enough, and puzzlement about what else is needed.

The fourth Enlightenment belief that is being questioned is the assumption that knowledge is inherently good. For centuries, science has been regarded as unquestionably a force for good. Today we are becoming increasingly aware that there is no inherent connection between knowledge and its beneficial use, with genetic engineering just beginning to open new possibilities of abuse and with the power of bombs and other destructive forces at hand.

These then are four reasons to say that the foundations of the modern world are crumbling and that we are becoming postmodern. In a postmodern world Christianity is intellectually relevant. It is relevant to the fundamental questions, Why does the world exist? and, Why does it have its present order? It is relevant to the discussion of the foundations of morality and society, especially as regards the significance of human beings. The recognition that Christianity is relevant to our entire society, and relevant not only to the heart but to the mind as well, is a major change in our cultural situation. The transition is hardly complete, but this is the vista which a postmodern world reveals.

So far, I have discussed the possibility of God and the need for God. I want now to turn to the experience of God. I shall examine our experience of God in the context of the second area of breakdown in the modern mentality, the breakdown of the foundations of morality and society.

In Christianity we claim that human beings are significant, indeed that they have indefeasible value. That is, our value cannot be annulled or undone. How can this claim be sustained? How can it be made convincing? How can it be brought within the range of our experience?

Classical western democratic theory claims that people have inalienable rights to life, liberty, and property. No government can violate these rights, or take them away from us justly.

Let us contrast this with the story of the Good Samaritan. A man is robbed, beaten, and left as a heap of battered flesh beside the road. A Levite and a priest pass by without helping. Do they violate the injured man's rights? No! Could they be said to have acted unjustly? No, not according to democratic theory. Yet Jesus once praised those who gave drink to the thirsty, fed the hungry, clothed the naked, and visited the prisoner. He called them just. They had performed acts of justice.

In the New Testament, the same Greek word is translated as "just" and as "righteous." The Good Samaritan was a righteous or just person. He performed a just act. This story reflects a different view of justice from that of western democratic theory. The New Testament view of justice is not limited to the protection of *rights.* Its view of justice is deeper, because it has a deeper view of what people are and the harm that can be done to them. This is why it seems strange to us to consider the act of the Good Samaritan as an act of justice. To those of us who think in terms of democratic theory, it is an act of mercy, not justice. But sense can be made of the New Testament view of justice.

The man who was beaten and robbed no longer had any possessions to cause anyone to take notice of him. He had no clothes to indicate his social position; had he been a person of distinction, perhaps notice would have been taken of him. Since his *relative* value could not be estimated (lying there as he was, naked), what claim did he have to consideration? If his claim is based on rights—if rights are the bottom line—then he has no claim. What applies to him applies to all of us. We can be left without family, money, friends. Talk to any refugee who has been reduced to nothing or who fears it. What basis does he or she have for making a claim on anyone? All such a person can do is to beg, to beg for mercy. People may listen or they may turn away. But no injustice is committed. That is, no injustice is committed *if* rights are considered to be the final and ultimate ground for a claim to consideration by others.

Our radical individualism in America is based on rights. We stress our freedom to do as we wish and resent restrictions. We speak as if rights, not obligations, are the bottom line.

The Good Samaritan story indicates that the bottom line is not rights. We do have a claim on others, and others have an obligation to us, because all of us have indefeasible value, value which cannot be annulled or undone. But in earthly terms, if we are stripped of all that we have—possessions and social standing—people can pass us by without committing an act of injustice.

But what gives us indefeasible value, if not our rights? We have absolute, indefeasible value because we have been made to participate in the life of God, and each of us is irreplaceable to him. The cry of the human heart in distress is met with silence when it turns to anything earthly. Only those who recognize in their own hearts the harm we can suffer, the anguish of what it is to be a human being in duress, can act as the Good Samaritan acted. They can see that it is *unjust* to allow that cry to be unanswered. They weep when they cannot answer it. They can recognize that it is an outrage to allow that brokenness to lie unnoticed or unattended.

Ernest Bevin, who led the dockworkers' union in Britain in the 1920s and 1930s, stressed that the most important goal of the labor movement was for the workers to gain a sense of human dignity and to stop feeling like second-class people. In the 1930s, a parliamentary commission was appointed to hear the case of the dockworkers. The management was represented by an eminent King's Counsel (a title of accomplishment in the legal profession). The dockers chose Ernest Bevin to put their case, even though he had little education and no legal or economic training. Bevin mastered the immensely complicated economic and legal facts relevant to the inquiry in a short time, and presented their case magnificently. He became known as the "dockers' K.C.," and it became a point of pride among the dockers that one of their own was able to make their case. These were people who knew humiliation and knew what it was to be restored to the level of personhood. That is what it is to experience graciousness, the graciousness of God.

We have learned from Arthur Miller that not only dockworkers can feel humiliated, but salesmen, too, can live a life of humiliation. In management as well, we are learning that humiliation must be endured in order to move up or to stay in place; dismissal can mean utter collapse.

In short, we ourselves can experience the reality of our indefeasible value when we recognize the horror of what it is to be reduced to a thing, something of which no notice need be taken. Without a Christian understanding of people we have no words with which to articulate the depth of that evil. Without Christianity all a person in duress can do is cry out and beg for mercy. There can be no appeal to justice and no way to articulate the horror that is being experienced except in cries.

Simone Weil brings out another feature of the New Testament view of justice by contrasting it to an incident recorded by Thucydides in his *History of the Peloponnesian War.* The small island of Melos sought to remain neutral in the war between Athens and Sparta. The Athenians sent an expedition to Melos and threatened the men with death and the women and children with slavery unless they would join them as allies. When the people of Melos cried out that this was unjust, the Athenians smiled and said that when two sides in a quarrel are roughly equal, some basis must be found by which an agreement can be reached. Then justice is appealed to. But when one side is strong and can get its own way, there is no need to take justice into account.

In Christianity, however, justice must always be considered, even when you deal with those who are weaker. You must always take others into account; not as a matter of mercy, but as a matter of justice, for there is an absolute equality between people. People are not equal in earthly ways, but our absolute equality is not based on earthly matters. The Good Samaritan treated someone who, on an earthly basis, did not have to be taken into account—who was a thing, a battered piece of flesh—as a person. By treating a man who had been reduced to a thing as a person, he restored him to personhood. Why did he do this? Because he could see the harm done, the horror of the reduction of a person—one made to receive God—to a thing. A theory of justice based on rights does not see this deeply into the harm done, nor into the need to restore a victim to personhood.

One of the great pitfalls of the present stress on rights as the bottom line is that, so often, it does not open our eyes sufficiently to the reality of good and evil. It can all too easily become the occasion for self-assertion and self-aggrandizement, *especially in those cases in which genuine injustice exists.* We are much more easily and frequently led into evil by what is good than by what is evil, for we feel utterly and perfectly justified in our cause. We then can fail to recognize the reality of others, especially our enemies. We fail to take them into account as having indefeasible value, and we thereby inadvertently violate the truth and reality of our own. The greatness of the civil rights movement of the 1960s was the way in which, Martin Luther King, Jr. and others stressed that the oppressor was not to be hated. The evil and injustice of white supremacy was made utterly clear, but so, too, was the indefeasible value of every person. This is what it is to do good and refuse to do evil. This is the way to justice.

The reality of good and evil forces a person to ask the question, How is evil to be removed? One of the convictions of the Enlightenment, and a pillar of the secular mentality, is that evil can be eliminated by improvements in the environment. It is claimed that people are antisocial because of social and economic institutions. Improve the institutions and you will improve people. Then with better people, better institutions can be devised. With still better institutions, even better people will be produced, and so on, until evil is completely eliminated. This is explicit in Marxism, which derived its texts from western theorists of the eighteenth century, the French philosophes. Whether or not it is seriously believed that utopia can be reached, the asssumption that evil is a function of institutions is present in much social theory today.

There is a lot of truth in the modern emphasis on the importance of institutions in relation to evil. For example, one of the problems with the power which science puts at our disposal is the lack of institutions to control its use. Scientists themselves have little control over the use to which their knowledge is put. Individual scientists have refused to work on some projects, but they knew at the time of their refusal that other scientists would be found to replace them, so that their action would only be symbolic. If a large number of a nation's scientists refused to cooperate on some defense projects, we know how easily that nation could be taken advantage of by a rival. So personal integrity is not enough. Some institutional organization is needed to control the power that science makes available. Institutions, then, are essential for achieving certain important ends.

Institutions are limited, however. Pascal puts it well when he notes that excellent organizations and social order can be built on human concupiscence.[4] By concupiscence Pascal means our longings, wishes, and desires for sensuous gratification and prestige or honor. He claims that no matter how noble a society's institutions may be, some appeal to personal gratification and prestige is needed to gain people's cooperation and so enable the institutions to operate. It must be worth our while to cooperate. But concupiscence can create only an image, at best, of genuine love or charity.[5]

Charity and concupiscence are different kinds of motives, but the results love achieves can be imitated or approximated by appealing to greed and prestige. A person can perform a task out of love alone; a person can perform the same task for money alone. The motivation is different, but the results may be very much the same. It is only when we come to rely on money alone as a motivation that we can slowly begin to notice a difference in the results, and realize that they are but an imitation of what love achieves. But organizations and society depend heavily on concupiscence for their continuation. Consider, for example, the airlines. The attention and coordination of mechanics, flight attendants, pilots, flight controllers, not to mention those responsible for food preparation and clearing the runways, is simply remarkable. The actions of hundreds of individuals must be carefully coordinated. The result of their actions is the safe transportation of travelers. But the coordination of activity is based on a system of compensation made possible by paid tickets; it is not based on love. It produces only an image of charity. Nothing dishonorable is implied in saying this. Indeed there is probably some extra effort here and there on the part of many of the people involved in making the airlines work. Still, the entire operation is only an image of charity.

Why does it matter what the motives are so long as the results are good? There are two reasons. They arise even when the results of an organization's operations are good, as in the case of the airlines providing safe travel. Let us consider education as an example. It is a challenge to live up to the aims of education with personal integrity. It is all too easy for an institution to penalize actions which promote genuine education, and to reward actions that do not. When this happens, people are caught in a bind. They are hurt or penalized if they act with integrity; but they suffer if they do not act with integrity, and suffer in proportion to their moral stature. Problems of integrity always arise because no organization's system of rewards and punishments matches perfectly the aims of education. So people who care about genuine education are always troubled with the problem of integrity. If they succumb to the system, they feel guilty. If they do not, and suffer the consequences, they may become angry and bitter.

The second reason why motives matter is that an organization's system of rewards and punishments can never create allegiance to the aims of education. A system of rewards and punishments may be largely in line with the aims of education, and so achieve some positive educational results, but it can never of itself create allegiance to those aims. In one way or another, the lack of allegiance to those aims will show in the results, just as an airline which depends solely on pay and prestige as rewards and punishment will not do as good a job as one that also has people conscientious working for it who do more than they are paid to do, or more than they are praised for doing. Greed and prestige can give only an image of charity, never precisely the same results as love.

Nonetheless, we cannot neglect the motives of greed and prestige. Classical Christian theologians, such as Augustine, have taught that the power of government to reward and punish is approved by God. The motives governments appeal to are crude, but a system of rewards and punishment that tends to promote the good of society can benefit us. Lower motives can be harnessed by the state as well as by other organizations to promote the good of society. But classical Christian theologians also point out that governments and social institutions only channel people's motives and restrain their impulses, thus producing an image of charity. They do not remove evil.

The removal of evil does not seem to be very important socially, as long as people behave and cooperate. The removal of evil then seems to be a private matter only. But unless there is some higher motivation at work within enough people in a society, its social institutions, and so the entire social order, cannot function well, no matter how much we reward and punish people's lower motives. A society which relies solely on greed and prestige loses even its image of charity. When too many people are concerned with themselves only, so that we can only appeal to lower motives, even the image of some goods cannot be achieved. Let's assume we own a business. We find ourselves spending, say, $60,000 a year, and not getting the results we once were able to get for $20,000 a year from people who had some concern for the goals of the organization. Then we find that it takes $100,000 to get the results we once got for $60,000. Sooner or later we find that we cannot afford to get a particular task done at all, or that there are simply not enough of the right sort of people available to maintain a former level of life, no matter how much money is spent. This certainly seems to have been a major factor in the decline of ancient Rome, and is perhaps beginning to be felt in our own society.

In a society that is in good working order, the social significance of good motives and the removal of evil is underrated. When a family is operating all right, the need for the removal of evil is not apparent. Only when a breakdown or crisis occurs is forgiveness recognized as important or even essential. So too for society at large. Organizations must rely on lower motives, however noble their aims. We have to be paid so that we may eat, however noble we may be and however much we care for the good of others. But if we think we can control people's behavior, and harness them to good aims, by appealing to lower motives only, then we are hiding from ourselves the guilt, anger, and bitterness which come from the problem of integrity, and the lack of allegiance of those who lack integrity. Even the image of charity will become impossible. Relying on the system of rewards and punishment built into an organization will not deal with evil and its corrosive effects. Some way to remove evil must be available.

How is evil removed? By contact with what is pure and good. Evil cannot remove evil. When evil strikes something that is itself not pure, it bounces back, often with an increment of evil, or it ricochets and hits someone else. Allow jealousy or envy to arise in an organization and watch its effects. Unless it is absorbed by some people who have sufficient goodness to overcome their natural reaction, jealousy and envy spread and grow. But a genuinely good person, instead of responding to evil with evil, absorbs it. Evil cannot soil genuine goodness and purity; it cannot defile it. It causes good people to suffer, but because of their suffering and their refusal to pass it on, evil vanishes. If there is enough goodness, any evil can be absorbed; if there is inexhaustible goodness, all evil can be absorbed.

Where is such goodness and purity to be found, and found inexhaustibly? In God alone. And God is not remote. His purity is present in those people who are in contact with him. It is even present to a degree in every person, since every person is made or formed in God's image. Every person has a degree of purity; if we pay attention to what is essential about persons and not what is personal, that very image of purity in another has the power to be cleansing in ourselves. God is also present in the beauty of the natural order of the universe. Nature can be a passage for God's purity to reach our senses and also our intellect. The actual study of nature by a scientist can be purifying. It can remove our evil, and precisely to the degree to which we love and respect the world. God is also present in the rites of the church. Those rites celebrate and make accessible to us the incarnate word of God, who came into the world and endured the suffering that evil causes, in his own person, and did not return evil for evil. In all of these ways we can experience the removal of evil. We can experience the presence of a gracious God.

Contact with God matters socially because the removal of evil restores those who fail to act with integrity and feel guilty, and it restores those who act with integrity but who are angry and bitter. It can free people to act with noble motives and seek to realize the aims of various institutions and organizations. Contact with God acts as a yeast in a loaf, as the salt which gives flavor to our social life. What is holy or pure is usually inconspicuous. We are not forced to take notice of it. We all too easily look only to what is powerful to save a society. But that one man of Galilee, the rites of the church (classified as a voluntary organization), and the beauty of the world (which is irrelevant to the advancement of scientific knowledge)—all of these have the power to remove evil and to raise our lives above the level of pedestrian and base motives. A society needs—every worthwhile

3. The Church's Mission to a Postmodern Culture

George A. Lindbeck

There are two ways in which this chapter may seem to depart from what its title suggests. First, it deals with the past and present more than with the future; and, second, it focuses on the Bible rather than on other culturally important factors in the church's life. Yet the topic remains in fact the same. Notions of the past influence visions of the future, and reconsideration of what has been goes hand in hand with reconceptualization of what is to be. When one looks at the past, however, the Bible is culturally preeminent. It has shaped the language and imagination of whole societies, and the question of Christianity's mission to postmodern culture is inseparable from that of the Bible's prospects.

I shall begin with some observations on the Bible's historic cultural role, and then turn to the dramatic weakening of that role inside and outside the churches in the recent past. Next I will discuss the consequences of that weakening and from there move to what, if anything, the churches can do about it. These first four parts of the chapter are a theologian's attempt at cultural analysis, but in the fifth section I shall conclude with specifically theological reflections.

I

Until recently, most people in traditionally Christian countries lived in the linguistic and imaginative world of the Bible. It was not the only world in which they dwelt. In most periods of Christendom, the poorly catechized masses lived also in a world of hobgoblins, fairies, necromancy, and superstition; in the educated classes, everyone, not least devout Christians, had their imaginations shaped by the pagan classics of the Greeks and Romans, to a degree we tend to forget. Further, from the days of Isaac Newton on, minds were also molded by modern science. Yet the text above all texts was the Bible. Its stories, images, conceptual patterns, and turns of phrase permeated the culture from top to bottom. This was true even for illiterates and those who did not go to church, for knowledge of the Bible was transmitted not only directly by its reading, hearing, and ritual enactment, but also indirectly by an interwoven net of intellectual, literary, artistic, folkloric, and proverbial traditions. We still speak colloquially of a Samson, or a Solomon, or a Judas, not to mention a Martha or a Mary. There was a time when every educated person, no matter how professedly unbelieving or secular, knew the actual text from Genesis to Revelation with a thoroughness which would put contemporary ministers and even theologians to shame. Even the deists and the atheists of the eighteenth-century Enlightenment, who for the first time made the high culture of the West avowedly non-Christian, were linguistically and imaginatively saturated with scripture.

This did not cease to be the case in the nineteenth and early twentieth centuries. Those who tried, like Nietzsche, to repudiate not only biblical beliefs, but the linguistic and imaginative universe of the Bible, nevertheless knew it well. Few escaped its influence. Marxism is not simply a secularized or this-worldly version of biblical eschatology, but that *is* part of its appeal; and, as recent studies indicate, the deep structures of Freud's thought were largely formed in interaction with his Jewish heritage, and John Dewey's, with his Protestant one. A familiar text can remain imaginatively and conceptually powerful long after its claims to truth are denied.

The scientific enterprise itself, even in the heyday of its warfare with religion, was often conceived in scriptural categories. Thomas Huxley, the great nineteenth-century advocate of science as a substitute for religion, argued for what he called "justification by verification." The phrase as he used it was weighty with Pauline and Reformation resonances. It is when we are trustfully obedient to reality as this speaks to us through the scientific method, not when we rely on our own words, dogmas, preferences, and prejudices, that we are justified. Further, much the same traits which evangelicals attributed to justifying faith, those of probity, responsibility, and love for humanity, flow from this justification by verification. Thus, in a scripturally literate culture, even the antiscriptural is biblically troped and colored. Christians need not be entirely unhappy with this misuse of their book. In Huxley's case, it led to an ennobling and ethnically strenuous view of science, and it is not clear that either scientists or society are better off now that the biblical trappings have been stripped away.

It is useful to comment further on the way in which texts influence human hearts and minds even when they are not believed. Once they penetrate deeply into the psyche, especially the collective psyche, they cease to be primarily objects of study and rather come to supply the conceptual and imaginative vocabularies, as well as the grammar and syntax, with which we construe and construct reality. They have many applications and therefore many meanings (as, indeed, was explicitly recognized in the old exegetical theories about the multiple senses of scripture). Thus, to take a nonbiblical example, Homer's *Odyssey* has functioned as a polysemous metaphor for a wide variety of adventurous journeys into distant times and places, and even into the hidden recesses of the mind. Not only literary but also scientific achievements can play a similar role, as becomes clear when we consider the figural and allegorical uses and misuses of Ptolemaic cycles and epicycles, the clockwork world of Newtonian physics, and the relativistic universe of Albert Einstein. Novels could also be cited. No one who has labored through Tolstoy's *War and Peace* will ever see the human scene in quite the same way again. Thus, texts of many kinds in many media, from unwritten myths to television projections, can become, as Calvin said of the Bible, the spectacles through which we see nature, human beings, and God.

Yet, to return to our main theme, the Bible has in this respect been preeminent in traditionally Christian lands. Its lenses have functioned as the most powerful, penetrating, and comprehensive ones. What has been seen through these lenses has varied widely, for they have been used to gaze on very different landscapes, on very different construals of reality. Yet each of these construals has acquired a biblical hue even when God is removed, as in the case of Huxley's argument. It is self-evident that the atheism which arises in historically Christian cultures cannot for a moment be confused with denials of the divine—for example, Buddhist ones—in other traditions.

So pervasive is this scriptural idiom that much of western literature consists of subtexts of the biblical text. This is true not only of obvious instances such as Dante's *Divine Comedy* or

Milton's *Paradise Lost,* but also of works such as Shakespeare's plays, which have little overt theological content. His comedies and tragedies are commentaries on life from perspectives structured by the biblically influenced culture in which he lived. He often surpasses even great theologians in his insights into what life looks like when viewed biblically, not because he knew the Bible better, but because he was a more acute and eloquent observer of the human scene. This telling of stories which exhibit biblical meanings is a way of explicating or commenting on the Bible itself: it is what the Jewish rabbis call midrash. There is a sense in which most of western literature is midrashic commentary; one does not have to be a Jungian to agree with the conclusion reached by Northrop Frye, one of the more prominant literary critics of this century, in his book *The Great Code:* that the basic substructure of the literary imagination of the West is biblical.

The outlines of that substructure are familiar, but it may be useful to recall them. Through most of Christian history, the Bible has been construed as a typologically unified narrative centered on Jesus Christ, in which all parts from Genesis to Revelation interact with all other parts. This interaction allows free play to imaginative intertextual and intratextual interpretations which are often not dissimilar to those of contemporary deconstructionists. Figuration and allegory are important, as well as midrash. Ordinary lay folk as well as preachers and theologians have engaged in the often gamelike activity of commenting on the biblical text by using it. In certain kinds of interpretation, such as the proverbial use of scripture, the populace has taken the leading role. Thus all of experience, including sacred texts from other religions, such as the classics of Greece and Rome, was absorbed into the scriptural framework. It is more than a metaphor, it is a literal description to say that Christendom dwelt imaginatively in the biblical world.

As I have already noted, this imaginative indwelling is a cultural phenomenon which can exist even where biblical beliefs are rejected or, more commonly, where the beliefs are nominal and biblical standards of behavior ignored. Being a cultural Christian is not the same as being a believing or behavioral one, and theologians have therefore generally treated it disparagingly. In the light of this disdain, it is worth recalling that this cultural Christianity, this linguistic and imaginative influence of the Bible, is not religiously unimportant. It has often been a condition for the communal shaping of convictions and conduct. Charlemagne in the eighth century was scarcely an exemplary believer, and yet he modeled his rule on that of a typologically Christianized King David, thereby laying some of the basic institutional foundations of western civilization (for example, the ideal—put into full practice only many centuries later—of free education for all those capable of and interested in learning to read). It has been suggested, to take another example, that the biblical allegory we know as *Pilgrim's Progress* did more to form the English noncomformist character than any other single factor. In this country, the traditions of black preaching may well be the most impressive recent instances of combined imaginative and behavioral use of scripture. As Henry Mitchell puts it,

The Black preacher is more likely to think of the Bible as an inexhaustible source of good preaching material . . . It provides the basis for unlimited creativity in the telling of rich and interesting stories, and these narrations command rapt attention while the eternal truth is brought to bear on the Black experience and struggle for liberation. The Bible undergirds remembrance and gives permanent reference to whatever illuminating discernment the preacher has to offer.

That sounds very much like a description of what the rabbis did, of early patristic exegesis, of how Luther spoke and wrote, and of much Puritan preaching. It is, one might say, the natural use of scripture when Christians have not not been spoiled by misconceived theology or science.

I am not, in this context, going to elaborate on why the traditional—and that includes the black preachers'—use of scripture has declined. Suffice it to say that after the Reformation the Bible became more and more exclusively an object of study with fixed and univocal meanings. It was no longer a language with many senses, a dwelling place of the imagination. Pietists were wary of any use except that of legitimating and evoking a particular kind of religious experience; legalists and social activists looked only for directives for personal or collective behavior; the rationalistically orthodox used the Bible as a proof text for unchanging propositional doctrines; fundamentalists argued about its scientific accuracy and their opposite numbers, the biblical critics, treated scripture as a set of clues for reconstructing what actually happened or was actually taught back in the days of Moses or Jesus. Traditional exegesis of the kind which prevailed through the period of the Reformation had been much more flexible. The Bible was studied in the ways just mentioned (even rudimentary historical criticism was not unknown), but above all scripture was used in endlessly varying ways to interpret the worlds in which the readers lived. The story of how this traditional exegesis disappeared among both conservatives and liberals would be the subject of another essay. It is the fact, not the causes, of the fading of the biblical component in western culture which must next concern us.

II

This fading involves a loss of both biblical literacy and biblical imagination. The two are not identical. As I have just noted in connection with pietists, fundamentalists, social activists, and historical critics, intimate knowledge of the text as an object can be dissociated from its use as a language with which to construe the universe. Yet, unless hindered by the rigidities on the right and on the left which hinder exegesis in modern times, knowledge and use naturally go together; and, in any case, knowledge, that is to say biblical literacy, is a precondition for any use whatsoever, whether imaginative or unimaginative.

The decline of biblical literacy is not to be confused with the growth of unbelief or of a secularized culture. The leaders of the Enlightenment, as I indicated earlier, were not believers, but they were biblically literate and biblically cultured. Conversely, Bible-believing fundamentalists sometimes know remarkably little of the content of scripture.

The decline of biblical literacy has been abrupt and pervasive. Language, culture, and imagination have also been debiblicized at a remarkable rate, not least in this country. The decline affects intellectuals and nonintellectuals, the religious and the nonreligious, those inside the churches and those outside, clergy and laity, and, as I just hinted, Bible-loving conservatives as well as purportedly less biblical liberals. In order to avoid misunderstanding, let me again stress that this is a de-Christianization of culture, not necessarily of society. At least in America, according to the Gallup poll, there has been no decrease of those who profess Christian beliefs, and the number of those who claim to be born again has increased.

Some examples are in order. Avowed secularists in the university at which I teach were considerably better educated, biblically, four decades ago than they are today. When I first arrived at Yale, even those who came from nonreligious backgrounds knew the Bible better than most of those now who come from churchgoing families. This ignorance of the Bible in the younger generation is a commonplace. A political scientist colleague told me not long ago that it is much more difficult now than in the fifties for students to understand even such non-Christian authors as Hobbes or Machiavelli. His younger faculty colleagues suffer from the same handicap: the biblical allusions escape them. We have probably all read the recent reports of widely used history school books which systematically omit reference to religion in their accounts of the past, and even tell the story of the first Thanksgiving without mentioning that it was a religious occasion, a thanksgiving to God. When I entered seminary, a knowledge of Bible content was presupposed and tested for at a level which now seems fantastically high. To be sure, there were self-proclaimed Bible lovers even in those days whose knowledge seemed limited to a handful of proof texts, but such people have now greatly increased in number. Perhaps that is one reason Billy Graham's popularity has declined: he presupposed greater biblical knowledge and was less casual about what the Bible actually says than are the Bible-thumping television evangelists who have succeeded him. Playing fast and loose with the Bible needed a liberal audience in the days of Norman Vincent Peale, but now, as the case of Robert Schuller indicates, professed conservatives eat it up.

The Bible, of course, is not the only victim of contemporary forgetfulness. American history, world history, and the corpus of

modernist, wholeheartedly agreed, and judging by their writings, if not by their professed beliefs, so also did James Joyce and most of the other major figures of the modernist literary canon. Their imaginations had been impregnated with scripture and the scripturally influenced heritage, even when they were anti-Christian.

Now, however, we are in a postmodern age. Authors steeped in the Bible are diminishing in number, and one cannot help but wonder about the future of the western literary tradition. But it would be wrong to think of this only as a literary problem. If imagination is basic to thought (as some modern cognitive psychologists, not to mention ancient Aristotelians, affirm), then the weakening of the biblical substructure of our culture's communal imagination may dry up the wellsprings of western humanistic creativity in general.

A second consequence is not unrelated to this first one, but is more tangible. With the loss of knowledge of the Bible, public discourse is impoverished. We no longer have a language in which, for example, national goals (that is, questions of meaning, purpose, and destiny) can be articulated. We try to deal with apocalyptic threats of atomic and ecological disaster in the thin and feeble idioms of utilitarianism or therapeutic welfare. Even an issue such as sanctions against South Africa gets trivialized by both opponents and supporters. It is hard to imagine any contemporary politician or even church leader declaring, as did Lincoln in his second inaugural speech, that God is judging and punishing not only the other side, the bad guys, the oppressors, but also the good guys, the side we favor, the freedom fighters. If Lincoln were to speak such words in our present situation, all the newspapers and television commentators would immediately assume that he was changing his mind, that he was going soft on slavery. But that was not the reaction of either believers or unbelievers in

North or South in the 1860s. Those who disagreed with Lincoln were sufficiently familiar with biblical modes of thought to understand what he meant.

Remnants of this skill were still with us a generation ago. Secular intellectuals had enough biblical background to find Reinhold Niebuhr interesting and challenging, and the whole nation responded to the scriptural resonances in the message of Martin Luther King, Jr. Could they have a similar impact now, a mere quarter of a century later? It is almost as if our society had forgotten how to use Arabic numerals and was forced to rely on Roman numerals. We would, for example, no longer have the concept of zero. Even simple multiplication and division would become formidably complex. Something like that seems to have happened to the idioms we use in discussing the great issues of the day. The culture of Christians as well as of non-Christians has been de-Christianized, and the language of public discourse has become dangerously feeble.

This brings us to a third and most palpable consequence. No single tongue has replaced the biblically influenced idioms of our past, not even a poor one. We have, in other words, no common language in which to discuss the common weal.

Lincoln, to cite him again as an example, did not call himself a Christian (or a non-Christian, as far as that goes), but he spoke to the whole nation in terms of sin and forgiveness, of God's judgment and mercy. The proslavery party resisted his message, but they understood it, and tried to reply in kind: that is, they sought to legitimate their position biblically. Now when it comes to discussions of apartheid in South Africa, there is a confusion of tongues among both conservatives and liberals. Utilitarian, therapeutic, and Marxist rhetorics confound each other. A common vernacular has even disappeared from the church. There are some on both sides who appeal to the Bible, to be sure, but the linguistic gap between apartheid fundamentalists and liberation theologians, for example, is vastly greater than that which divided evangelical abolitionists in the North from their nonabolitionist fellows in the South. In the Civil War period, incomprehensible as this now seems, Christians who shot at each other with intent to kill did not excommunicate each other. Most Protestant denominations divided along North-South lines, to be sure, but they regarded each other as genuine Christians, even if misguided, and were not averse to communing together at the Lord's table when circumstances allowed.

It seems that nothing like this is now possible. Society as a whole, and to a large extent the church also, has become a communicative basket case. Genuine argument is impossible, and neither agreements nor disagreements can be probed at any depth. Manipulation of public opinion with the threat of coercion from the right and of repressive toleration from the left becomes stronger and stronger, and the still small voice of reasoned argument which once could be counted on to play a moderating role (even in the midst of a Civil War) now has no common language in which to express itself.

Whether a society or civilization can survive under these circumstances is an open question. Every major literate cultural tradition up until now has had a central corpus of canonical texts: Homer and Virgil in the classic Mediterranean world, the Confucian classics in China (and, to a large extent, also in Korea, Vietnam, and Japan), the Bhagavad Gita in the lands influenced by Indian culture extending as far as the island of Bali, the Pali canon in Therevada Buddhism, the Koran in Islam, the Hebrew scriptures by themselves or supplemented by the New Testament in Judaism and Christianity. I suppose one could add the Marxist canon for communist countries except that this attempt, unprecedented in world history, to move directly from theory to practice, from communist ideology to communist society and culture, seems to be dying stillborn. All that seems to be left behind when revolutionary fervor cools are repressive regimes. In any case, if communism succeeds, it will be a further illustration that a common culture and language require a common canon. Without a shared imaginative and conceptual vocabulary and syntax, societies cannot be held together by communication, but only by brute force (which is always inefficient, and likely to be a harbinger of anarchy). But if this is so, then the biblical cultural contribution, which is at the heart of the canonical heritage of Western countries, is indispensable to their welfare, and its evisceration bespeaks an illness which may be terminal.

IV

In discussing the possibility of revivifying classic texts I will be brief. New opportunities are being created by the current intellectual shift towards what some people have characterized as postmodernity, and it is this shift that I want to discuss briefly.

Modernity has been deeply prejudiced against treating a classic as a language or lens with many meanings or uses with which to construe reality and view the world. Instead, as I have already suggested, modernity viewed texts primarily as objects of study, and that meant, among other things, that they were possessed of a univocal meaning, a single meaning ascertainable only by specialists, by historical critics for example.

All of this is now changing. What might be called the textualization of reality is apparent in figures as diverse as historians of science, such as T. S. Kuhn, and literary theorists, such as Jacques

Derrida. We find it natural, as previous generations did not, to speak of encoding data, following scripts in scientific investigations, and inscribing reality in texts. The sharp division between the natural sciences and humanistic studies is breaking down. One hears exacting scholars, as I did at a recent Smithsonian consultation, casually remark with the authority of the commonplace that the epistemological grounding of a physicist's quarks and a Homer's gods is exactly the same. It is rhetorical force rooted in forms of life which gives them different cognitive status. In our society, of course, quarks win by a wide margin over Homeric gods.

I shall refrain from discussing whether plausibility is lent to this denial of universally privileged epistemic and interpretive standpoints by Ludwig Wittgenstein's language games and W. V. O. Quine's webs of belief, or Richard Rorty's pragmatism. Whether these or other justifications of current developments are valid or invalid, the point is that the developments are taking place. The intellectual climate is changing, and the one we are now entering is congenial to the close reading of texts in order to see what the world looks like in and through them. For the first time since the Renaissance and Reformation the regnant outlook in the intellectual high culture is not opposed to treating a classic, whether Christian or non-Christian, as a perspicuous guide to life and thought.

As I have already indicated, it is questionable that the churches can seize the opportunities that this intellectual shift provides. But we have said enough to indicate how this might be done. Biblical literacy, though not sufficient, is indispensable. This literacy does not consist of historical, critical knowledge about the Bible. Nor does it consist of theological accounts, couched in nonbiblical language, of the Bible's teachings and meanings. Rather it is the patterns and details of its sagas and stories, its images and symbols, its syntax and grammar, which need to be internalized if one is to imagine and think scripturally. And when one proceeds to imagine and think scripturally, one may in fact use very little actual biblical terminology. What is to be promoted are those approaches which increase familiarity with the actual text. Even profane close readings of the canonical sources, such as are now becoming popular in a few English literature departments such as the one at Yale, are to be preferred to theology, however liberating, edifying, or othodox, which turns attention away from scripture.

Relearning the language of scripture is difficult, and at present there are no signs that the churches can do it. Forgetting rather than relearning is still the major trend. Yet if the direction were reversed, the cultural consequences might be considerable. We need not be a believer, I have been arguing, to think biblically about many things. And if the faithful led the way, others might follow.

One reason for thinking this could happen is the lack of effective alternative modes of public discourse. Robert Bellah and his associates have reminded us of the defects of the regnant American idioms—those of what he calls utilitarian and, more recently, expressive individualism. These languages even lack the concept of the common good. Their major worldwide rival, the Marxist way of speaking has, in addition to its possible internal flaws, been discredited for many by Marxist praxis. If, then, Christians were to employ their own language, not some other tongue, to address the problems of this society as it actually exists, not as it is fantasized by Christian reactionaries or Christian revolutionaries, they might find themselves helping to fill a cultural vacuum at the heart of national life. There are no signs that this will happen, but it could, and if it did, the church's postmodern cultural service to human need would be immense.

V

In this section I offer some final thoughts that are more specifically theological. So far everything that I have written could be written by someone who is not a Christian believer. It is tempting to stop and end with a call for Christians to take up their cultural mission and turn unlikely possibility into actuality, but there are theological questions which must be raised before we end. The problem is that Christianizing culture is both important and dangerous. It is, from one point of view, a biblical imperative, even though there is no command in the Bible to do so. The Great Commission does not speak of Christianizing cultures. It speaks of going and baptizing and teaching all nations. It is imperative, however, because cultural needs may be at times as urgent as physical ones and, furthermore, in one sense are more basic. Postmodern men and women do not easily survive in what for them is a cold and empty universe clothed only in the abstract jargon of sociological and psychological reason. If they wrap themselves, as Thomas Huxley did, in borrowed biblical metaphors, Christians have reason to rejoice and to think that providing the metaphors and keeping them in good working order is part of their Good Samaritan role. Furthermore, without the biblical shaping of the social mind and imagination, some societies, at least traditionally Christian ones, are likely to be even less just, less compassionate, less caring for the stranger then they would be if they had never been Christian. Nazism was not a reversion to Nordic barbarism, but far more savage. When Christian influence lapses, seven devils worse than the one originally expelled may well rush into the swept and garnished emptiness. As we earlier noted, Christian charitable social and political action on behalf of the poor and the oppressed can sometimes be effective only where there is already Christian cultural influence. Yet it can be disastrous to seek this influence directly. Unlike some other religions, a Christianity faithful to its origins does not seek cultural and the consequent social power.

Ambitions of this kind are forbidden to the servants of a crucified Messiah. And it was the forgetting of this prohibition which was the great sin of the Church during the age of Christendom. Not only did it acquire influence; that in a sense was inescapable, but it sought to promote and maintain that influence by worldly means. It forgot that Christendom itself was an unintended consequence of the early church's success in attending to its own communal life and language. It forgot that only when the songs of Zion are sung for their own sake will they be sung well enough to gain currency in society at large. The cultural mission cannot be programmed but is, from the human perspective, an accident or by-product of the Christian community's faithfulness in attending to its own language and life which, of course, includes service to others.

What the cultural mission is from God's perspective is another matter. He used the church to Christianize cultures in the past (it seems to me that it's a theological error to think of the age of Christendom as simply an aberration, not part of God's plan for his world), and perhaps he will do so again. Yet, on the other hand, there is no guarantee, either scriptural or nonscriptural, that God will do anything of the sort. Perhaps the de-Christianization of our society will continue to its quite possibly bitter end. Perhaps no new Christian cultures will emerge in Africa, Asia, or the Islands of the Sea, though in some ways I'm more optimistic about them than about traditionally western Christian lands. Perhaps the church of the future will lead an increasingly ghettoized existence in shrinking enclaves and unfriendly societies. We simply do not know. Of only one thing are Christians assured. God has promised to be with his people as judge and savior both in the catacombs and on the throne, and for either of these destinies believers need a mastery of their native tongue which is at the moment fast disappearing. Relearning the language of Zion is imperative whatever the cultural future of the church. And if some of us want to relearn that language, and I'm among the number, not simply in order better to sing God's praises but also out of concern for the societies in which we live, God will perhaps forgive us. Paul pointed out that there is reason to rejoice even when the gospel is preached for unworthy motives. And I for one am willing to pray that the same holds true for the promotion of biblical literacy in our society.

4. Does the Bible Have a Postmodern Message?

Sandra M. Schneiders

In his chapter, George Lindbeck has described the eclipse, if not the definitive demise, of biblical language as the imaginative source of world-construction in modern culture. I am forced to agree with him that contemporary western culture is no longer steeped in and shaped by the Bible as it once was. I suspect there are at least two reasons for this situation, which makes me ambivalent, if not pessimistic, about the possibility of reversing this phenomenon in the foreseeable future.

First, we must recognize the general failure of our educational system to transmit the classical tradition, including its Judeo-Christian religious component, to the several generations of students who have been the objects of so-called universal education. It is not only the Bible which these students do not know; they do not know Greek and Roman mythology, Plato or Aristotle, the classical poets, Shakespeare or Dante. But, in a political system which is nearly paranoid about the separation of church and state, knowledge of the biblical tradition is doubly a victim: as a classic the Bible is largely neglected; as a canonical religious document it is virtually proscribed. Therefore, if knowledge of the Bible is to saturate the imagination, if the language of the Bible is to provide the linguistic lenses through which reality is viewed, it is the Church which must educate the mind, the tongue, and the sensibility of society.

This brings me to the second reason for the eclipse of the biblical tradition, namely, that the churches have in large measure failed to offer to young people a religiously satisfying version of Christianity. Thus, spiritually hungry youth have turned elsewhere, e.g., to the East, to the cults, or just to drugs, for the framework of meaning within which to structure their existence in this world. Even those who have been led by circuitous routes to re-examine their own religious tradition do not approach it tabula rasa. They tend to merge what they vaguely remember or finally learn of Christianity with what they already know of eastern or other religious doctrine and practice, in a kind of symbolic mélange which does not allow the biblical tradition to exercise a controlling influence on their imaginations. Even if religion eventually becomes important for them in their construction of world and self, biblical Christianity is not the exclusive or self-evidently superior religious resource that it might have been for their forebears.

And yet, as Albert Outler recently pointed out in his article on postliberal hermeneutics,

the Bible remains as a unique focus of interest and inquiry: to believers and non-believers, to historians, literary critics—"to all sorts and conditions" of men and women. . . . The aim of a postliberal hermeneutics is to reposition Holy Scripture as a unique linguistic medium of God's self-communication to the human family. . . . as the human medium of a divine revelation that has endured and will endure in and through the cultural metamorphoses that succeed each other as history unfolds.[1]

I can only agree, on the basis of personal and professional experience, that there seems to be, at least among Roman Catholics who have come newly, after four hundred years of famine, upon the promised land of sacred scripture, an unprecedented interest in conferences and summer sessions on the Bible, in articles and books of *haute vulgarisation* that provide a reliable but readable entrée to the biblical texts, and in the use of scripture for personal meditation. If, as Professor Lindbeck has suggested, the best way for the Church to influence culture is through fidelity to itself, by doing what it is supposed to do, namely, transforming its own members into a truly biblical people, then I think all is far from lost. If anything, we are engaged in a period of biblical renewal in the postconciliar Church.

However, these biblically formed Christians will bring into the contemporary cultural mix of twentieth-century America *one* voice, *one* view of reality with its challenges and problems, and not *the* view as in a time when citing scripture sufficed to establish the rightness of one's position or at least the righteousness of one's intentions. Reality, even for the believing and biblically literate Christian, is not spontaneously construed by and through biblical categories and language. Those who would see the world biblically must work to do so and work even harder to make their vision readable and compelling to others. I am not certain that this is an altogether lamentable state of affairs. It might well mean that the biblical worldview has ceased to be the going *ideology* and has become instead a *dialogue partner* worthy of respect only if it offers something better than what is attainable by other means, and only if those who propose it are better because they espouse it than they would be without it.

In short, we are no longer a Judeo-Christian or biblical culture but a pluralistic, postliberal culture in which the biblical world-view is a minority position. As Karl Rahner pointed out over a decade ago, we are in the process of becoming again a Church of the "little flock," a Church in diaspora.[2]

Whether or not this is a disaster is a matter of critical opinion. Perhaps it could be argued that the Church is being recalled from a sixteen-century-long Constantinian exile, from a cultural domestication to which we in the west have been too long accustomed. Perhaps the Bible, in ceasing to belong to the lingua franca of the land, and thus to function as an instrument of cultural imperialism, will become again the challenging address to freedom it was meant to be.

REFRAMING THE QUESTION

This much having been said, let me reframe the question with which we began: Does the Bible have a postmodern message? I see the question not in terms of whether the Bible's cultural-linguistic hegemony can be recovered, but in terms of two other questions. First: given the fact that we are, thanks to the Enlightenment, definitively beyond the spiritually enriching but scientifically underdeveloped, more-than-literal, exegesis that was characteristic of the patristic and medieval periods,[3] and that we seem to be coming to the end of the reign of the characteristically modern approach to scripture, namely, historical criticism,[4] can the Bible continue to *mean* in a postmodern world? In other words, is there a new way into the text which can allow it to be religiously meaningful for our contemporaries? I will try to suggest that the answer to this question is a confident yes.

Second: as the oppressive use of scripture to legitimate the historical victimization of the poor by the rich and the oppressive content of scripture as a patriarchal document become ever more clear under the analytic inquiry of contemporary ideology criticism, can the Scriptures continue *to claim the allegiance* of postmodern Christians? On this question the jury is still out. I will try to describe some of the options that are currently under consideration, and offer an evaluation of their prospects.

BEYOND MODERN EXEGESIS: A NEW HERMENEUTICAL APPROACH

Let me briefly, and perhaps much too simplistically, describe what I call the modern approach to the Bible. Historical criticism approaches the biblical text as an object to be studied according to the model of objective scientific understanding that emerged from the Enlightenment and was applied to the interpretation of texts by nineteenth-century romanticism.[5] The text, in such a model, is to be analyzed with all the tools of the "higher criticism," including not only philology but also modern literary and historical methods. The primary objective of such analysis is to derive from the text historically accurate knowledge about the persons, events, and religious understandings of the ancient times in which the texts were produced and about which they spoke. Under the influence of this ideal, the exegesis of the Bible has become in the course of the last century an ever more specialized discipline, and the results of that study ever more tentative and arcane. The Bible seemed to recede further and further from the grasp of the ordinary Christian and to become the property of the scholars who alone and with great difficulty could decipher it. And what the scholars uncovered seemed to become less and less spiritually nourishing even as it became more historically accurate. The scholars seemed to be caught in an infinite historical regress, tracing the ever more remote explanation of the ever more fragmented text into an ever receding antiquity that was ever less relevant to the concerns of the contemporary believer.

Needless to say, there were many pastorally responsible biblical scholars who worked hard to bridge the gap between ancient text and modern community and to make the results of scholarship available to believers in religiously meaningful terms.[6] But the process of pastoral application remained a second-order operation in which scientific knowledge of what the text "really" meant was somehow translated into modern terms and applied to the contemporary Christian.[7] The inviolable distinction between what the text actually meant, i.e., what was intended by its ancient author and understood by its original audience, and what the text might mean for a contemporary audience, made the process of application an essentially extrinsic operation that often left the modern believer alienated from the revelatory encounter which brought him or her to the text in the first place. But for both pastoral and academic reasons the reign of historical criticism as the controlling if not sole approach to biblical interpretation seems to be coming to a close.

Academically, the turn to language characteristic of contemporary philosophy as well as developments in literary criticism are having a powerful influence on biblical scholarship.[8] Scholars are coming to realize that the locus of revelation for the contemporary Christian is not the events behind the texts, nor the theology of the biblical authors, nor even the preaching of the texts in the community, but the texts themselves as language that involves the reader.[9] The focus of interest is not so much on what produced the biblical texts as on what the texts, when fully engaged, produce in the reader. Thus, the positivistic objectification of the text which resulted inexorably in the dilemma of the subject–object paradigm of understanding by analysis has begun to give way to a hermeneutical paradigm of understanding by participative dialogue. Interpretation, in other words, is not a matter either of dominating the text by method or of submitting to the text in servile fideism, but of entering into genuine dialogue with it as it stands. Through this dialogue reader and text are mutually transformed. The reader is transformed not by capitulation but by conversion; the text is transformed not by dissection but through multiple interpretations to which it gives rise by its surplus of meaning, but which can only be actualized by successive generations of readers whose interpretations enrich the texts themselves.[10]

Pastorally, historical criticism seems to have run its course as an independent religious resource. This is emphatically not to say that historical criticism has no place in biblical research and therefore in the preparation of pastors for the work of announcing the Gospel. Indeed, even the nonprofessional reader of scripture is ill-advised to dispense in a cavalier fashion with the results of scientific criticism. But it is to say that those who would facilitate the revelatory encounter between text and believer must go beyond the admittedly indispensable philological and historical preparation for understanding the text, and learn how the text functions as language. Language, especially the biblical language, is not a semantic container in which theological information is stored and delivered for consumption. Language is the medium through which the event of transformative understanding takes place. Learning to deal in live metaphors, to let parables ensnare, subvert, and enliven, to find the symbols that function in our culture and to use them to religious ends;[11] in short, to operate in and through language as the Bible itself does is the newly rediscovered task of the preacher.

To claim that we are witnessing the end of the era in which the scientific paradigm of biblical interpretation, historical criticism, held unchallenged sway in both academy and church is to say that we are entering a postmodern period of biblical scholarship and preaching.[12] The promise of unlimited and finally definitive knowledge of most if not all of the Bible's meaning has not been fulfilled because it was not fulfillable. Revelation is not primarily, much less exclusively, a matter of more or better knowledge, but of deeper and richer encounter. We have learned a great deal about scripture, just as we have learned a great deal about society, the human psyche, and the universe. This knowledge is not to be disdained, but it is also not enough. Scientific criticism is necessary, but it is not sufficient. Just as we are finding new ways in science, ways that do not denigrate or neglect the solid achievements of the modern period but which go on to complement those achievements by an appreciation of values, of the specifically human, of the holistic and the integral, so must we find new ways in biblical interpretation. It will not be easy for those of us reared in the intellectual milieu of the modern period to feel confident or at ease with the less quantitative methods and less measurable results of these new approaches. But the signs, as I read them, are very hopeful.

BEYOND OPPRESSION: THE BIBLE AND THE CHALLENGE OF LIBERATION

This brings me to my second question: given the contemporary discovery of the oppressive content of much of the Bible and the ideological uses of the Bible throughout history to legitimate and support the domination of the weak by the strong, can the Bible continue to claim the allegiance, to function as revelatory medium, for the people of a postmodern world? The answer to this question is, as I have suggested, much less clear and it is to this question that I wish to address more extended attention.

The question involves two problems: the ideological *use* of Scripture, which is, if you will, an exterior problem; and the ideological *content* of Scripture, which is intrinsic to the text.

LIBERATION THEOLOGY IN GENERAL: SCRIPTURE AS RESOURCE FOR THE OPPRESSED

The question of the *use* of scripture for the purposes of oppression is being focused in the third-world struggle of the poor for liberation from domination by the rich and for participation in the societies and cultures which have been, for so long, controlled by the economically powerful for their own advantage. The struggle involves wresting the sacred text from those who have used it to legitimate their oppressive regimes and strategies and delivering it into the hands of the oppressed as a resource for liberation. While there are many problems, both academic and pastoral, with the way scripture is being interpreted and used in third-world and black liberation theologies, the basic analysis of the oppressive use of scripture by the dominant classes and the repudiation of that use seems quite sound.[13] Furthermore, the consciousness-raising appropriation by the oppressed of the biblical myths and metaphors of liberation and of the prophetic message of both Testaments is serving as a resource for the struggles of blacks in this country, of peasants in Latin America, of the victims of apartheid in South Africa.[14] The problem of the ideological use of scripture is soluble and is slowly being solved.

LIBERATION THEOLOGY IN PARTICULAR: FEMINIST CRITICISM AND
HERMENEUTICS

The second problem involved in our question, that of the
ideological *content* of Scripture, is much more complicated. It is
being focused in the struggle of women for liberation from
patriarchal oppression in family, society, and church, and in the
struggle of feminists, both men and women, to destroy the patriarchal ideology which grounds not only sexism but racism, classism, clericalism, and all the other forms of dualistic hierarchy in
which the powerful dominate the weak in the name of God. Here
the problem is not that scripture has been *used* to legitimate
oppression (although this is a continuing problem) but that the
Bible itself is both a product and a producer of oppression, that
some of its *content* is oppressive.

The Bible was written in a patriarchal society by the people,
mostly men, whom that system kept on top. It embodies the
androcentric, that is, male-centered presuppositions of that social
world, and it legitimates the patriarchal, that is, male-dominant,
social structures that held that world together. Its language is
overwhelmingly male-oriented, both in reference to God and in
reference to people. In short, the Bible is a book written by men
in order to tell *their* story for *their* advantage. As such, it con-
fronts both women and justice-inspired men with an enormous
problem. It is not at all certain that the Bible can survive this
challenge, that it can retain the allegiance of people called to
justice and freedom in a postmodern world.[15]

The issue of biblical patriarchalism is essentially twofold: there
is the question of patriarchal ideology and the question of male-
dominant language. I will discuss the first and not the second. But
I do not wish to imply by omission that the question of language

is a minor or frivolous one. As Professor Lindbeck has insisted, language is that by which we construe and construct our world. To the extent that women are invisible in biblical language, they are nonparticipants in the biblical construction of reality. To the extent that they are degraded by that language, they will continue to be oppressed in the Christian community.[16] But let us turn to the even more fundamental issue of patriarchal ideology in scripture.

Patriarchy is a social–economic–political system in which the head of the social unit (family, tribe, clan, nation, church, plantation, etc.) is seen as the divinely established and absolute owner and ruler of the social unit, including all its members and parts.[17] Because this head in the basic social unit of the family has been, at least in the west, the father–husband, there is a close connection among maleness, power, ownership, and domination on the one hand and femaleness, powerlessness, poverty, and subjection on the other. Because society has been ruled by male heads of social units there has been a natural assumption that maleness was the normative mode of humanity, resulting in the unconscious but powerful androcentrism, or male–centeredness, of western culture that is both reflected in and reenforced by the male–generic patterns of virtually all western languages.

It is important to realize that the patriarchal family was viewed as the divinely established model for all other social units and patriarchy, i.e., male hierarchy, as the necessary principle of all social order. Thus, the king in his realm, the Pope in Christendom, the pastor in his parish, the plantation owner with his "darkies," the colonial power bearing "the white man's burden" for childlike primitives, were all versions of the adult male father figure, the "holy father" who was naturally, and by divine right, superior to and responsible for the inferiors God had entrusted to him. His rights to dominion could not be questioned without challenging God "Himself," who was the ultimate divine patriarch and who willed to establish order in society through father rule modeled upon "His" own dominion. While the patriarch was answerable to God for the way he exercised his dominion, and called by noblesse oblige to exercise it benignly, he was in no sense accountable to those he owned and ruled, any more than God is accountable to humans.

What contemporary ideology criticism has uncovered is the intrinsic connection among all forms of systemic domination. The nerve of classism, racism, colonialism, sexism, and clericalism is patriarchy.[18] One of the most important legacies of the modern period is the successive challenging of all systemic embodiments of patriarchy. The French and American revolutions definitively undermined the principle of divine right monarchy; the Protestant Reformation repudiated the divine right papacy; the Civil War and the civil rights movement in this country challenged the divine sanction of slavery and white supremacy; the anticolonial movements in Africa, India, and now in Latin America have tackled intersocietal classism; various labor movements throughout the world have challenged the superiority of management based on wealth and power.

But as we well know, discrimination has not vanished. The rich continue to dominate the poor; ethnic majorities persecute members of minorities; clerics continue to claim divine prerogatives, and so on. In short, patriarchy is far from dead. And one of its most ubiquitous and still basically unquestioned forms is raw sexism, the domination of women by men, not just because the women are poor, or black, or lay, i.e., members of patriarchally dominated groups or classes, but simply because they are female. The attempt to raise a systematic challenge to sexism has proved a slippery undertaking at best. The efforts to obtain the vote for women, to assure their right to all roles and responsibilities in the Church, to outlaw discrimination in school and on the job, to have rape and incest regarded as serious and punishable crimes rather than as boyish excesses or male familial rights, in short, to establish the equality of women as persons and under the law in family, society, and church have met with massive resistance and ambiguous success.

Women are well aware that one of the most powerful allies of patriarchy in general and sexism in particular is the biblical text.[19] The Bible was written in a patriarchal culture and reflects the assumptions of that society. It assumes that history is the story of important men and their exploits and so to a large extent it omits, obscures, and distorts the participation of women in sacred history. It assumes the human and moral inferiority of women and so regularly reduces them to their biological roles in relation to men and demonizes their initiatives. It assumes male superiority and so legitimates the sexual double standard within and outside of marriage and winks at male violence against women. And this says nothing of such explicitly oppressive injunctions as that wives submit to their husbands (compare Ephesians 5:22–24) and keep silent in the Churches (compare 1 Corinthians 15:34–35). We are not speaking of an occasional text that could be explained or explained away but of a pervasive patriarchy, androcentrism, and overt sexism that directly and indirectly, by what it says and what it fails to say, lends the authority of sacred scripture to the age-old oppressions of patriarchy and particularly to the oppression of women by men.

As contemporary liberationist criticism, and particularly feminist criticism, lays bare the ideological presuppositions and content of the biblical text, various publics are responding in different ways. At one end of the spectrum are men and women, mostly of fundamentalist bent, who read the text literally and accept its presentation of male superiority as normative for their individual and community lives. Indeed, some even rejoice in the idolatry of maleness and the subordination of women that it seems to enjoin.

At the other end of the spectrum are an increasing number of women, among whom are many of the best-educated and most socially committed, who have decided that the Bible is such an oppressive and degrading text that no woman of integrity can espouse it as revelatory and continue to live with self-respect and develop toward human wholeness.[20] These women have abandoned Christianity for post-Christian alternatives, either as separatists or as part of feminist-based communities of women and men. Their departure is both a loss for Christianity and a challenge, for they incarnate the inevitable ultimate result of the failure of the community to deal with this problem.

In between these two extremes are those women and men who, under the impetus of feminist biblical hermeneutics, are trying to find a way to deal with the biblical text which will be both faithful to the sacred text and liberating for women. Feminist hermeneutics is a multiform movement in the biblical academy which defies easy definition and manifests itself in extremely diverse interpretive practices. In general, the feminist interpreter starts from the premise that only that can be accepted as God's true revelation which supports and promotes the full and equal dignity and personhood of women. The task then becomes how to deal with a sacred and canonical text which contains much that does not meet that criterion.

The earliest feminist interpreter of the Bible, Elizabeth Cady Stanton, solved the problem by excising from the Bible those texts which were oppressive of women. Modern interpreters recognize that this approach is self-defeating and have taken other paths.[21] Some, like Rosemary Radford Ruether, who invokes the prophetic tradition of divine liberation from oppression, have appealed to a "canon within the canon" to allow the biblical text to criticize and correct itself from within. Others, like Phyllis Trible, have tried to use the tools of rhetorical and literary criticism to reveal the fullness of the divine plan for humanity that is inaccessible to historical criticism in its fixation on factuality.[22] Still others, like Elisabeth Schüssler Fiorenza, have used a sophisticated form of historical criticism itself to reconstruct the experience of the early Christian community, using the text's very omissions, negativities, and unintentional revelations to restore women to Christian history and their Christian history to women. Other scholars have undertaken to deal with particular theological and spiritual issues in the text, such as the masculinity of the God image, the maleness of Jesus, the patriarchal character of Church order and the like. Still others have concentrated on finding and reinterpreting the female figures of sacred history who have been obscured by a masculinized theological, liturgical, and homiletic tradition,[23] or retelling, in memoriam, the "tales of terror" in scripture in which hatred and violence against women have been enshrined.[24]

As yet, none of these approaches individually, nor all of them together, have succeeded in reclaiming the Bible for women, but they are opening up new approaches to the text while, at the same time, raising fundamental questions about how and in what sense the biblical text is revelatory. It is not certain that the text can be saved; but it is certain that it cannot be saved as a simple container of revelation or literal transmitter of divine truth. Furthermore, feminist hermeneutics has made it clear that revelation cannot be equated with history in the sense of what actually happened, nor can the Bible be considered, without further ado, as a normative archetype for contemporary Christian life. In short, the questions that are being raised by liberation theology in general and feminist criticism in particular are not merely concerned with how the oppressed can relate to a patriarchal text but, more fundamentally, how the Christian community can appropriate its sacred literature in a postmodern world. Unless I held out some hope that we would find an answer to this question, I would long ago have abandoned the field of biblical scholarship. But unless the Church as a whole takes this entire issue much more seriously than it is currently doing, I and others like me may be forced to conclude that the Bible does not have a life-giving message for the postmodern world but belongs definitively to an age in which the domination of some humans by others could appear to be a God-given right. Only a hermeneutics which effectively weds the best of the new forms of criticism with a genuinely liberating interpretation and praxis can allow the Bible to function as Word of God within a postmodern context.

NOTES

1. Albert C. Outler, "Toward a Postliberal Hermeneutics," *Theology Today* 42 (October 1985), 281–91; see esp. p. 286.
2. See, for example, Karl Rahner, *The Shape of the Church to Come,* tr. E. Quinn (New York: Seabury, 1974), esp. pp. 29–34.
3. For an interesting re-appraisal of precritical biblical exegesis, see D. C. Steinmetz, "The Superiority of Pre-Critical Exegesis," *Theology Today* 37 (1980), 27–38. R. E. Murphy, in "History of Exegesis as Hermeneutical Tool: The Song of Songs,"

Biblical Theology Bulletin 16 (1986), 37–91, concludes that earlier methodology enriches historical-critical work.

4. See P. Stuhlmacher, *Historical Criticism and Theological Interpretation of Scripture: Toward a Hermeneutics of Consent,* tr. R. A. Harrisville (Philadelphia: Fortress, 1977), for a brief history of the method and a proposal for going beyond it without repudiating it.

5. For a brief analysis of nineteenth-century developments in hermeneutics, see R. E. Palmer, *Hermeneutics: Interpretation Theory in Schleiermacher, Dilthey, Heidegger, and Gadamer* (Evanston: Northwestern University, 1969), 75–123. See also the analysis of H. G. Gadamer in *Truth and Method.*

6. A monumental effort in this direction is *The Jerome Biblical Commentary,* ed. R. E. Brown, J. A. Fitzmyer, and R. E. Murphy (Englewood Cliffs: Prentice-Hall, 1968). See also numerous more popular commentary series.

7. See the classic formulation of this position in Krister Stendahl's article, "Contemporary Biblical Theology," *The Interpreter's Dictionary of the Bible,* ed. G. A. Buttrick et al., Vol. I (New York: Abingdon Press, 1962), 418–32.

8. For a brief overview of new approaches, see T. J. Keegan, *Interpreting the Bible: A Popular Introduction to Biblical Hermeneutics* (New York/Mahwah: Paulist, 1985) or J. Barton, *Reading the Old Testament: Method in Biblical Study* (Philadelphia: Westminster, 1984).

9. See, e.g., Gail R. O'Day, *Revelation in the Fourth Gospel: Narrative Mode and Theological Claim* (Philadelphia: Fortress, 1986).

10. See Mary Ann Tolbert, *Perspectives on the Parables: An Approach to Multiple Interpretations* (Philadelphia: Fortress, 1979), for both a theoretical presentation and a practical example.

11. An outstanding practitioner of this art is Amos Wilder. See, e.g., his *Jesus' Parables and the War of Myths: Essays on Imagination in the Scriptures,* ed. J. Breech (Philadelphia: Fortress, 1982). See also W. Brueggemann's *The Prophetic Imagination* (Philadelphia: Fortress, 1978).

12. On the character of the modern and postmodern mind sets, see Huston Smith, *Beyond the Post-Modern Mind* (New York: Crossroad, 1982), esp. pp. 132–61.

13. Cristine E. Gudorf, "Liberation Theology's Use of Scripture; A Response to First World Critics," *Interpretation* 41 (1987), 5–18.

14. Some excellent popular texts have appeared in recent years. See, e.g., the remarkable work of A. Nolan, *Jesus Before Christianity* (Maryknoll: Orbis, 1978).

15. For a very clear analysis of the problem, see Mary Ann Tolbert, "Defining the Problem: The Bible and Feminist Hermeneutics," *Semeia* 28 (1983), 113–26.

16. I have treated this issue at some length in *Women and The Word: The Gender of God in the New Testament and the Spirituality of Women* [Second Annual Madelva Lecture in Spirituality] (New York/Mahwah: Paulist, 1986).

17. For a good analysis of patriarchy as a principle of social organization, see W. A. Visser t'Hooft, *The Fatherhood of God in an Age of Emancipation* (Geneva: World Council of Churches, 1982), esp. chapters 1–3.

18. Rosemary Radford Ruether has been a leader in unmasking this connection. For a brief readable presentation, see her "Feminists Seek Structural Change," *National Catholic Reporter* 20 (April 13, 1984), 4–6.

19. The leading analyst in this area is Elisabeth Schüssler Fiorenza. See her *In Memory of Her: A Feminist Theological Reconstruction of Christian Origins* (New York: Crossroad, 1983), esp. chapters 1–3.

20. The outstanding representative of this position is Mary Daly. See her *Beyond God the Father: Toward a Philosophy of Women's Liberation* (Boston: Beacon, 1973), which was the magna carta of this movement.

21. See Schüssler Fiorenza's treatment of the approach of Cady Stanton's *The Woman's Bible* in *In Memory of Her,* 7–14.

22. See Phyllis Trible's *God and the Rhetoric of Sexuality* (Philadelphia: Fortress, 1978).

23. Cf. Elisabeth Moltmann-Wendel, *The Women Around Jesus: Reflections on Authentic Personhood,* tr. J. Bowden (London: SCM, 1982).

24. Phyllis Trible, *Texts of Terror: Literary-Feminist Readings of Biblical Narrative* (Philadelphia: Fortress, 1984).

5. Christian Faithfulness in a Pluralist World

Robert N. Bellah

Epiphany is a season when we reconsider the central issues of our faith, for in Epiphany, Christians think about the manifestation of our Lord; the disclosure, in a series of events, of who he is, but also of the words that make him known, which are present in many of the Gospel readings during Epiphany. It is in Epiphany, for example, that we hear the voice from heaven at his baptism saying, "This is my beloved Son, in whom I am well pleased," and John the Baptist saying, "Behold, the Lamb of God," and Jesus himself saying, "Repent, for the kingdom of heaven is at hand." These are disclosing words, creative words, words that create a world, and we Christians must utter such words and hope that they will disclose something real. It is also during Epiphany that our lectionary contains the Sermon on the Mount, an extraordinary disclosure of Jesus himself, but also an extraordinary disclosure of the art of teaching and preaching, to which I will return.

In this essay I will be very much concerned with the issues set forth by George Lindbeck, both in his book *The Nature of Doctrine,* and in his chapter in this volume. I am concerned with how we can recover biblical language and Christian practice within the community of the faithful. I agree with Lindbeck that we have largely lost our fluency in the biblical tongue and that it is not easy to see how we can regain it. This is in part because we have been caught up in the cacophony of other tongues which we have had to learn, and our biblical language has been pushed to the periphery. We might call this the problem of pluralism, the multiplicity of tongues that we moderns are required to speak. But I will argue that modernity gave us a false pluralism and that we must now seek to grasp a genuine and therefore a postmodern pluralism. Thus though "postmodern" is not in my title, this chapter, like the others in this volume, is concerned with the postmodern condition.

I will argue that modernity has given us a false pluralism because it has claimed to offer a new metalanguage which is really true, and to which all the particular languages of culture and religion must be reduced. The new metalanguage is the language of facts, proven by scientific method to be truly, objectively there. Most of us, including most of those in the pews of our churches, give an unthinking priority to the world of scientific fact as the world of the really real. Of course we know that facts are not everything, that there are also feelings that are subjectively present in ourselves and others, and that we must take feelings seriously (though not quite as seriously as facts) or we may suffer unpleasant consequences. In *Habits of the Heart* my coauthors and I called the languages of fact and feeling "utilitarian and expressive individualism" and suggested that the combination of these two ways of speaking is our "first language," our dominant view of reality.

This situation presents the members of our churches and synagogues with a quandary, for the language of the Bible is not divided neatly into facts and feelings, and indeed the Bible conceives of reality in ways quite alien to our conceptions of objectivity and subjectivity. The hegemony of the first language of modernity is indicated by the fact that many believers unconsciously accept its primacy and so must translate the language of faith into the language of modernity. This they can do in several ways. The fundamentalists translate the Bible into the language of fact and thus make of it a scientific document. The religious liberals translate it into the language of feeling, thus endowing the Bible with "psychological truth," which means that it isn't really true but that it is psychologically supportive.

Needless to say both of these are ways in which we cease to understand, and so cannot adequately speak, the language of the bible. For those of us who are preachers or teachers faced with parishioners and students for whom the language of modernity is obviously true and the language of the Bible, untranslated into the universal Esperanto of modernity, is obviously not, the problem of disclosing what the Bible is saying seems almost insurmountable.

But while the laity is blissfully confident of the language of modernity, the language of fact and feeling, some of the most influential contemporary intellectuals and philosophers no longer accept its self-evidence. Indeed, even science itself is no longer seen as a collection of objective universal truths, but rather as a set of research traditions carried by particular communities of inquirers, and unintelligible outside the lived practice of such communities. We imagine, not only most of the laity but those of us who preach and teach as well, that what we take to be the scientific worldview is simply the way the world is. We do not see, at least unless we think about it carefully, that it is a socially constructed world, provided to us by a scientific community.

Further, we take the world on faith. We all know that the earth goes around the sun rather than, as appears, the sun goes around the earth. Only children and primitives make that mistake. But how many of us are able to prove that the earth goes around the sun? It is because of our confidence, our trust, our faith in the scientific community that we believe it, not because we, in the strong sense, really know it.

And our socially constructed conception of how things really are is seriously out of date. We are Newtonians in an Einsteinian world. We unconsciously believe in a world of endless uniform extension in time and space. But the world of contemporary physics is one in which space and time are curved, have a beginning, and probably an end. In other words, time and space are more local and particular, more peculiar, than we imagined, even if the distances involved are unimaginably great. My point is not that modern physics proves the biblical worldview—that would be to fall into the modernist trap, for tomorrow science may prove something entirely different. My point is that only those actively engaged in studying these things really know why one way of looking at them is superior to another.

And looking at science in this way, as philosophers and historians of science have come to do during the last couple of decades, we discover that science is not so importantly a matter of proven facts, though such facts seen in a larger context are certainly essential, as of fundamental conceptions of how things are, of visions, we could even say of disclosures. The great scientist is one who sees in a new way, and when he sees in a new way he is often despised and rejected by other scientists. The facts he adduces to support his vision are not even seen as facts by those locked in another paradigm. Historians of science sometimes speak of conversion to a new paradigm. Often scientists past a certain age never are converted, never do see the new paradigm, and go to their graves devoted to the old way of thinking. And those who are converted are so because they have taken up the scientist with the new vision as an exemplar, have accepted his definition of the problem, and are actually practicing a research program based on his work.

The conclusion I draw from this new way of thinking about science is that although science is alive and well, scientism, which is another way of designating the first language of modernity, is seriously undermined. The actual practice of science does not warrant the claim of scientism to be a universal language superior in its validity to all the beliefs and practices of mankind. Rather, science turns out to be just one more "tribal tradition," or set of tribal traditions, whose validity must be tested in the general discussion and practice of human beings. Scientism turns out to be not the fact that it proclaims itself to be but a fiction. Or rather, what we really have to learn is that the difference between fact and fiction is not what we thought it was. Remember that fact and fiction, as might be apparent even from the sound of the words, both come from the same Latin root, *facere*, to make. Both facts and fictions are "made things." Their validity does not derive from the objective truth of facts or the subjective truth of fictions, but from how they actually operate in the living practice of human beings. If scientism is fiction as much as fact, a myth and not a very good myth, it is because, as the basis of living human practice, it has chaotic results. The very way in which it divides fact and feeling deprives morality of any objective validity and reduces it to a matter of subjective feeling, to what Alasdair MacIntyre has called emotivism, leading to an ethical wilderness in which the good is whatever any of us feels it is, and

moral argument either is interminable, degenerates into a shout-
ing match, or is decided by force. Scientism turns out to be an
ethos that legitimates the war of all against all and cannot produce either an ethic or a spirituality.

Once we take the measure of the limitations of modern consciousness we may begin to look at Christianity in a new way.
No longer need we think of it as a set of sentimental fictions that
we tell to children or to ourselves when our feelings are hurt.
Rather, Christianity is the living practice of the Christian community, a way of educating simultaneously our intelligence and
our feelings so that our actions may be rightly guided in accord-
ance with the example of the one whose life is the basis of all
that we do.

But what I have tried to show so far—namely, what kind of
thing Christianity is; that it is not a set of sentimental fictions but
the language and practice of a living community—is only half
the battle, or maybe far less than half. For to participate in the
Epiphany today, to make Christ manifest, to disclose the truth
for our lives of what was incarnate in him, we must show what
he was and what he means for us now. If our contemporaries,
including many of the ostensible believers, do not understand
what *kind* of thing Christianity is, they certainly do not understand nor do they want to understand *what* it is and what it asks
of us. Not that it is ever easy even for those of us who have made
it our task to try to understand it and communicate it.

The Church has chosen over the centuries to meditate on a
number of events during the season of Epiphany that have the
quality of manifestation: the star of Bethlehem that was discerned
by the magi, the baptism of our Lord, the wedding at Cana, and
that most mysterious event, the transfiguration. But the manifestation that I want to consider is Christ as preacher, the living

Word preaching the living word. I want to take as my example a great Epiphany text, the opening of the Sermon on the Mount, those singular verses we call the Beatitudes, an extraordinary disclosure of Jesus himself, but also an extraordinary disclosure of the art of teaching and preaching.

Let me insert here some moderately encouraging information for those of us worried about the decline of biblical literacy. According to Dr. George Gallup, whereas in 1954 only thirty-four percent of Americans knew who delivered the Sermon on the Mount, in 1982, forty-two percent knew the right answer. Incidentally, in 1954, thirty-five percent of Americans could name all four gospels, whereas in 1982, forty-six percent could. And whereas in 1944, ten percent of Americans were daily Bible readers, in 1984, fifteen percent were. Not stunning testimony to biblical literacy, but the trend is encouraging.

If we do not merely repeat the words but take the Beatitudes seriously and truly grapple with what is being said, then we will soon be shocked to discover that this great proclamation of the good news will come to most Americans as very bad news indeed, for it goes against our central beliefs. We may remember that at the end of the Sermon on the Mount, Matthew writes, "And when Jesus finished these sayings, the crowds were astonished at his teaching . . ." If we are able to open ourselves, even a little, to the original power of the Beatitudes, and not be mesmerized by the familiarity, or the archaic unfamiliarity, of the words, I can guarantee you that we will be astonished too.

"Blessed are the poor in spirit, for theirs is the kingdom of heaven." Immediately we are hit with the difficult, seemingly self-contradictory phrase, "poor in spirit." Does it mean "spiritually humble" so that rich people who don't think too well of themselves can be "poor in spirit"? Well, by extension it can certainly mean the spiritually humble, but, say the commentaries, if Matthew had simply meant "humble" he had perfectly good Greek ways of saying so. Certainly the word "poor," whatever its metaphorical uses, refers to the actually, materially, poor. Luke in a parallel passage says simply, "Blessed are the poor." Rather, poor in spirit seems to mean those who are really poor but are untroubled about it, uncomplaining about it. We might even go so far as to say that they accept permanent defenselessness and insecurity. And what does this archaic word "blessed" mean? Well, one of its plain meanings is "happy." The Jerusalem Bible translates it, "Happy are the poor in spirit . . ." And so Jesus is starting right out in the first sentence of the greatest sermon ever preached telling us that the really poor who are untroubled by their poverty are happy, and further that "the kingdom of heaven is theirs." That is, present tense, they are now already participating in the messianic fulfillment that it was Jesus's special mission to bring about on earth. Now almost nobody in America is going to want to hear that.

The conservatives will wonder why these poor folks are so happy. Don't they have any ambition? Don't they know this country is a land of unlimited opportunity, where the children of the poorest immigrants can become governors, senators, and CEOs of our largest corporations? And besides, if there is going to be any kingdom of heaven on earth certainly it should belong to those who have worked hard and deserve it and not to poor people who are so apparently lazy that they are satisfied with their poverty.

Nor will the liberals like it any better. Why should the poor be happy? Don't they know that it is the rich who are oppressing them and keeping them down? And how can they be enjoying the kingdom of heaven now when we haven't yet reformed the social system so as to eliminate poverty? The liberal may even feel that a passage like this proves the Marxists are right; that Christ was just trying to keep the poor happy while the rich could go on being rich, when what he should have done is exhort us to do something about poverty. Elsewhere, of course, he did exhort us to do something about the poor: to feed them, clothe them, take them in. But not here. Here he is trying to shock us, to open us up to something we don't want to see, to disclose to us a reality different from the one we take for granted.

Or let's take the second Beatitude: "Blessed are those who mourn, for they shall be comforted." Those who mourn are those who suffer loss, perhaps those who have lost everything. To put it in present American parlance we might think of those who mourn as "losers." But what kind of un-American thing is Jesus saying? That losers are happy and will be comforted, when we all know that ending up a loser is the worst thing that can happen to you and that you certainly won't be happy?

Or what about the meek in the third Beatitude? "Meek" is another somewhat archaic term that Richmond Lattimore translates as "gentle." Certainly it means unaggressive. The unaggressive are not only happy but they are going to inherit the earth? Whoever heard of such a thing? Everyone knows that it is only the go-getters, the really aggressive, who ever get anything on this earth, and certainly if we want global power it is only armed might that will get it. Jesus, as we would put it in California, seems to be completely off the wall.

I have been able only to begin to unfold the depths of meaning in the first three Beatitudes and show how powerfully, how shockingly, they will speak to us if we will only hear them. I cannot here even do that for the next five, which consider those who hunger and thirst for righteousness, the merciful, the pure in heart, the peacemakers, and those who are persecuted for righteousness' sake, though each one of them would richly repay careful exegesis.

Let me skip, then, to the last Beatitude, the ninth, where there is a dramatic shift that puts the whole passage in a new light. But first let me point out that the first eight Beatitudes are an example of what I said at the beginning of this chapter about words creating a world. For the first eight Beatitudes create a world just as surely as the word of God in Genesis 1 creates the heavens and the earth and all that is in them. The first eight Beatitudes create the world of the heavenly kingdom. Note the symmetry of the first and eighth Beatitude: both conclude with "for theirs is the kingdom of heaven." The first eight, with remarkably compressed power, follow a fixed third-person declarative form: "Blessed are the . . . , for they shall. . . ." But suddenly, in the ninth Beatitude, Jesus shifts to direct address: "Blessed are you when men revile you and persecute you and utter all kinds of evil against you falsely on my account. Rejoice and be glad [the King James Version says, "be exceeding glad"], for your reward is great in heaven, for so men persecuted the prophets who were before you." Jesus has saved the greatest shock for the last. We are to be happy when men revile us and persecute us. We are to rejoice and be glad when they utter all kinds of evil against us. For his sake. When we are doers of the word and not hearers only. And by the very form of the language he has moved from creating the world of the heavenly kingdom to addressing us directly and pulling us, as it were, into that world. The participation in the messianic kingdom in and through Jesus Christ, who *is* the kingdom incarnate on this earth, brings a joy and a gladness that overwhelm all the sufferings of the world.

What Jesus is teaching is an affront to more or less all of the cultures in human history, but to none more so than our own. We have, probably more than any culture in history, emphasized competition, survival, and success. Perhaps only in America could someone say and be respected for saying, "Winning isn't everything, winning is the only thing." But Jesus is saying it doesn't have to be that way. Life does not have to be lived as a harrowing struggle for survival with the honors going to the foremost. Those who haven't "made it" don't deserve to be despised and neglected and those who have "made it" don't need to be so desperately anxious about constantly achieving more. Instead Jesus holds up to us the poor, the outcast, the rejected, the persecuted as the place where the kingdom of God is, where *he* is (the Last Judgment passage in Matthew 25 where Jesus tells us that as we did it to the least of these we did it to *him*). Bishop Lawrence, Episcopal Bishop of Massachusetts in 1901, said that "Godliness is in league with riches . . ." (I wonder where he found that in the Bible), but Roger Williams in the seventeenth century was closer to Jesus when he said, "the Godly are persecuted and the more Godly the more persecuted." In that regard we can think of Martin Luther King, Jr., or of Archbishop Tutu and his co-workers in South Africa today.

So if we listen well, we will probably, like the crowds gathered on the mountain, be "astonished at his teaching." We may even, with God's grace, be able to see through these words a glimpse of our incarnate Lord. But will it make any difference? Will it transform our lives? Will it be as the seed that is sown in rocky soil in the parable of the sower, that flourishes for a moment but withers as soon as the sound of the words has died away? If all we have is words, important as language is, that is probably what will happen. But we have more than words.

George Lindbeck has indicated that the churches with a strong liturgical tradition have a special advantage in that the biblical teaching is carried in the practice, the enactment, the embodiment, of the liturgy.

The compressed message of the Beatitudes is enacted each time we jointly celebrate the Eucharist: "On the night he was handed over to suffering and death, our Lord Jesus Christ took bread; and when he had given thanks to you, he broke it, and gave it to his disciples . . ." In the Eucharist we have a powerful and central enactment of the kingdom of heaven, the reign of God. It should be a focal action, a focal practice, that radiates out into the whole of our lives. But again, does it really happen or does the power of the Eucharist remain imprisoned in the walls of the church for the brief time that we come together to celebrate it?

In chapter nine of *Habits of the Heart* we describe an Episcopal parish, St. Stephen's Episcopal Church, where, partially and uncertainly to be sure, the power of the Eucharist, of the kingdom of heaven, does break out into the whole lives of its members. They are actively concerned with the hungry and the homeless. As members of the East Bay Sanctuary Covenant they may well be persecuted. We cannot take any special pride in that example, however, because American congregations show a wide range of spiritual vitality. Yet it is strengthening for us to remember that there are churches not only in America but all over the world, where the word is not only preached but where, in the light of the word and the sacrament, Christian communities are actually living a life of discipleship, enacting the parables of Jesus, showing forth the reign of God, losing their lives as they find them in him.

On the other hand, it is a chastening experience to read the description of Faith Episcopal Church in *Varieties of Religious*

Presence, by David Roozen and his associates. Faith Episcopal glories in its Anglo-Catholic liturgy. It doesn't use the 1979 Book of Common Prayer or even the 1928 version, but sticks to its nineteenth-century prayer book. It is one of those inner city parishes that survives with a commuter congregation. As one observer put it, "it physically and liturgically resembles a beautiful but hidden garden, tucked away from the working-class neighborhood surrounding it." The same observer wondered why some of the neighbors don't throw a rock through the windows of the iron-fence enclosed church which has so little concern for its surroundings. A 1969 parish survey concluded that Faith Episcopal has "something very valuable that we want to preserve and that the world needs very much," but that they didn't see how to share it. Roozen notes that it is no different today and reports that the rector is looking forward to an upcoming sabbatical.

But in the same book there is a description of a Roman Catholic parish, St. Margaret's Church, that has a very similar sacramental theology to Faith Episcopal, but with very different consequences. St. Margaret's parishioners are largely Hispanic and live in the poorest neighborhood of Hartford, Connecticut. Its priests have led it into active involvement with social issues, but it is its focus on the Eucharist that gives it its strength. As one member put it:

The Mass is the reenactment of the moment of Redemption. In every Mass, the Cross of Calvary is transplanted into every corner of the world, and humanity is taking sides, either sharing in that redemption or rejecting it, by the way we live. We are not meant to sit and watch the Cross as something done and ended. What was done on Calvary avails for us only in the degree that we repeat it in our lives. All that was said and done and acted during Holy Mass is to be taken away with us, lived, practiced, and woven into all the circumstances and conditions of our daily lives.

A deacon indicates that life at St. Margaret's "begins and ends with the Mass." Priests and people agree that, as the pastor puts it, "Mass is the center of everything." He goes on to say:

The eucharist is the living presence of Christ. In sharing that presence, the call is to go out and make that presence operational, living in the world. That going out wears us out, so the eucharist is both the beginning and the end: It draws us to it, pushes us out into the world, and then draws us back. It is an overflow of the Lord's presence. The Mass is part of the world and the world is part of the Lord.

Bible study is an important feature of the life of St. Margaret's. The large youth group, for example, meets every Sunday evening to study the Gospel lesson for that week. It is one of the results of Vatican II that Catholics are becoming more Bible-oriented and, reciprocally, many Protestants are becoming more liturgically focused.

The new Catholic emphasis on the Bible is nowhere more evident than in the recent pastoral letters of the American bishops, especially the letter titled "Economic Justice for All." This is in marked contrast to the famous 1919 letter that began the American Catholic tradition of social teaching, which is almost completely devoid of biblical reference. This change too might be of some comfort to George Lindbeck. I would like to discuss this recent letter in detail and show how its fundamental principles of solidarity, participation, and subsidiarity are rooted in the Bible and a profoundly trinitarian theology. But here I will only use the letter as a touchstone to my next major point. At several places in the letter the bishops make the point that we are called as Christians to a variety of immediate actions to help the poor, such as assisting with soup kitchens and shelters for the homeless, but that our obligation does not end with such immediate acts. We are also called, they say, as citizens, to act through the public political process so that the whole society takes responsibility for its problems.

The bishops do not give a biblical justification for their emphasis on citizenship, but Father John Coleman, a Jesuit and a leading Catholic sociologist, recently has. Father Coleman, in an unpublished paper, has developed a fascinating analysis of Romans 13, that often troubling passage that seems to legitimate all the powers that be, by pointing out that it is surrounded at the end of chapter 12 and from verse 8 of chapter 13 by assertions of the Christian ethic of neighbor love as powerful as Paul ever wrote. Paul was not living in a world in which Christians had power, yet he asserts the validity of the political order and exhorts the Christian to engage in acts of charity. We might also remember that Paul himself claimed Roman citizenship, an act that can hardly be seen as condemning the political and judicial process of his time. The inference to be drawn from all this is that discipleship and citizenship, though often in tension, are both valid obligations for Christians.

Yet in the society in which we live, true citizenship is as badly understood as true discipleship. Where we can casually utter the oxymoron "the private citizen," we don't know what citizenship is. In other words, we need to retrieve the language of citizenship just as we need to retrieve biblical language. And it is the same monoculture of fact and feeling that has endangered biblical language which makes the language of civic republicanism hard to understand. For if the truth about human beings is that they are radically self-oriented interest seekers, then there is no such thing as the common good and politics is a disguised form of warfare, contained only by certain operating rules of procedure. The retrieval of a genuine language of citizenship, rooted in the practice of the ancient polis and of the best periods of our own history, would be a contribution to that genuine pluralism that I have argued is only possible in a postmodern world. Another metaphor for this process would be the replacement of a situation in which the universal Esperanto of modernity dominates, with a few half-understood polyglot survivers hanging on, by one in which we would become genuinely multilingual, speaking the language of science and psychology where they are appropriate, but also speaking the language of the Bible and of citizenship, unashamedly and well. It is because of the possibility and indeed the necessity of such a genuine multilingualism that George Lindbeck's proposal does not lock us into a narrow parochialism or a new sectarianism, as at least one of his critics has implied. My last point is that following Lindbeck does not close us off to the pluralism of the world's religions either. Just because, following his metaphor, we can learn languages other than our own, it is possible for us to learn something of the language and practice of another faith, even though we never become a native speaker, or, to vary the metaphor, even though we remain visitors in those other houses of faith. I am aware of the temptation of shallow dilettantism. Having spent much of my life in the study of Japanese language, culture, and religion, I know that any genuine encounter is hard won and partial at best. Lindbeck himself has shown us how, by following his method, we may better understand other Christians and in principle Jews and Muslims as well, for they share with us much of the same basic vocabulary. Lindbeck indicates that dealing with the eastern religions that share none of our assumptions will be more difficult. I am not so sure. Especially since there has been a long history of conflict and disputation the differences, in one sense minor, that separate us from our siblings and our cousins may be more threatening and make mutual understanding more difficult than when we are dealing with those who are, so to speak, strangers (though I don't think there is such a thing in human culture and religion as *total* strangers).

I would argue that it is important for us to understand, through partial participation in them, the religious worlds of other faiths, both for developing the crucial mutual understanding so needed in the contemporary world, and also for our mutual spiritual enrichment. Probably most Christians will not have the time and energy to do this at all, and none of us can seriously encounter more than a very few other faiths, but it is important that we have among us those who know the religious traditions of other human beings.

Let me illustrate my argument with an autobiographical example. As part of my Japanese interests I have long been concerned with Mahayana Buddhism, and in particular with Zen. Not only have I read a great deal in that tradition, for some years now I have been visiting the Zen Mountain Monastery at Tassajara for brief summer retreats and have engaged in zazen there. In 1986 the San Francisco Zen Center, of which Tassajara is a part, invited me to become one of two "outside" members of its board. The other was Brother David Steindl-Rast, a Camaldolese Benedictine who lives at New Camaldoli, the Hermitage of the Immaculate Heart, at Big Sur, on the coast just a few miles west of Tassajara. Brother David and I were glad to serve because we believe that this community, which has recently been going through difficult times, is a serious expression of the spiritual life and has much to contribute to all of us both as Americans and as Christians. Their effort to live a life of committed community focused around an ancient religious practice, in great material simplicity, close to the soil of our California landscape, giving a nonviolent witness to the larger society, seemed to us to have exemplary value.

I was particularly moved, when in the summer of 1985 I took my retreat at the Benedictine Hermitage rather than at Tassajara, to see that in the hour after the evening Eucharist when the monks and guests sat in an hour-long contemplation of the elements of the sacrament, many of them sat in the posture of zazen. This implied no syncretism and no weakening of Christian commitment. It was a simple borrowing of a valuable cultural element from one tradition by another, of a sort that has been going on for millennia to the great spiritual enrichment of us all.

In conclusion, however, I want to return to George Lindbeck's basic call for us to recover the integrity of our own faith and its lived expression. I hope that we can live in a more truly pluralistic, genuinely multilingual, world. But if we do not recover the language and practice of Christianity, if we do not discover that the kingdom of heaven is our only true home, the place that defines our most essential identity, then not only can we not contribute to a genuine pluralism, but we will be lost in the wilderness of decayed traditions and vulnerable to the domination of modernity's suicidal infatuation with power, the exact opposite of the Gospel message. I agree with Lindbeck that our greatest contribution to the world is to try to be who we are. That effort will never be easy and will probably bring upon us rejection and persecution, but it will also make us exceedingly glad.

6. Postmodern Theology and the Judgment of the World

Rowan D. Williams

In the nineteenth century, Kierkegaard retold the story of Abraham and Isaac with shattering effect; several generations have grown up spiritually and intellectually in the shadow of this retelling in terms of the "suspension of ethics," the realm of risk and terror beyond morality. More recently, Jung in his *Answer to Job* reworked the scriptural text into an extraordinary new mythological shape: the blind God of the natural and primal order looks with envy at the creature who has the self-awareness to challenge him; the conflict between Job and his maker shows why that maker himself must at last identify himself with human suffering, must become Jesus Christ. Only as human is God self-aware; only as human is God fully God, the active and transfiguring archetype of the human itself.

What is going on here? Should we call these enterprises translations of the world's experience into biblical categories, or the opposite? It is because I find I am not at all clear about the answer to this that I want to put some questions to the project so persuasively outlined by Professor Lindbeck in his book, *The*

Nature of Doctrine, and in his chapter here, the project of inserting the human story into the world of scripture: "Intratextural theology redescribes reality within the scriptural framework rather than translating scripture into extrascriptural categories."[1] I have no doubt at all of the need to revive and preserve a scriptural imagination capable of deploying decisive and classical narratives in the interpretation of the human world—nor any doubt of the present weakening of such an imagination in our culture. But I am both interested and perturbed by the *territorial* cast of the imaginary used here—of a "framework" within whose boundaries things—persons?—are to be "inserted." Is this in fact how a scripturally informed imagination works? I believe that the reality is more complex, and that it sits less easily with the picture Professor Lindbeck has outlined of a church heavily committed to the refinement and deepening of a scriptural speech and culture *within* its own territory.

What I shall be proposing is that we may have misunderstood the alternatives before us. The "world of scripture," so far from being a clear and readily definable territory, is an *historical* world in which meanings are discovered and recovered in action and encounter. To challenge the church to immerse itself in its "text" is to encourage it to engage with a history of such actions and encounters; and in the era after the disappearance of a unitary Christian worldview, this is to engage with those appropriations of biblical narrative on the frontiers of the Church and beyond represented by figures such as Kierkegaard and Jung.[2] If, as has sometimes been said, the Bible is itself a history of the *re* reading of texts, our reading of it should not be so different. What we are dealing with is a text that has generated an enormous family of contrapuntal elaborations, variations, even inversions—rather like the simple theme given to Bach by Frederick the Great, that forms the core of *The Art of the Fugue.* When we have listened to the whole of that extraordinary work, we cannot simply hear the original notes picked out by the King of Prussia as if nothing had happened. We can't avoid saying now: *"This* can be the source of *that"*—and that is a fact of some importance about the simple base motif.

The Church may be committed to interpreting the world in terms of its own foundational narratives; but the very act of interpreting affects the narratives as well as the world, for good and ill, and it is not restricted to what we usually think of as the theological mainstream. Something happens to the Exodus story as it is absorbed into the black slave culture of America. Something still more unsettling happens to Abraham and Isaac when they have passed through Kierkegaard's hands—or the hands of the agnostic Wilfred Owen, writing in the First World War of how the old man refused to hear the angel "and slew his son, And half the seed of Europe, one by one." Where are we to locate this kind of reflection? It is not purely intratextual, conducted in terms fixed by the primal narrative, nor is it in any very helpful sense a "liberal" translation into an extraneous frame of reference. It is, much more, a generative moment in which there may be a *discovery* of what the primal text may become (and so of what it *is*) as well as a discovery of the world. Owen's savage transformation of Abraham's sacrifice points up what we might miss in Genesis: the final drawing back from slaughter is an act of obedience as great as or greater than the first decision to sacrifice Isaac. It also points up the impotence of the narrative in a world that has lost the means to forego its pride. Not sacrificing Isaac is a necessary humiliation; the righteous old men of Europe in 1914 are strangers to such a possibility. This is indeed a discovery of scripture and world, and of the gulf between them; and it is now—or should be—part of what the Church reads in Genesis 22. It will have found out *what it is itself saying* in absorbing this scriptural exegesis from its own margins. And part of my thesis is that the interpretation of the world "within the scriptural framework" is intrinsic to the *Church's* critical self-discovery. In judging the world, by its confrontation of the world with its own dramatic script, the Church also judges itself: in attempting to show the world a critical truth, it shows itself to itself as Church also. All of which means that we are dealing not with the "insertion" of definable blocks of material into a well-mapped territory where homes may be found for them, but with *events* of retelling or reworking traditional narrative patterns in specific human interactions; an activity in which the Christian community is itself enlarged in understanding and even in some sense evangelized. Its integrity is bound up in encounters of this kind, and so in the unavoidable elements of exploratory fluidity and provisionality that enter into these encounters. At any point in its history, the Church needs both the confidence that it has a gospel to preach, and the ability to see that it cannot readily specify in advance how it will find words for preaching in particular new circumstances.

Words like "preaching" and "interpretation" have come to sound rather weak; or, at least, they do not very fully characterize the enterprise to which the Church is committed. The Church exists for the sake of the kingdom of God; it is "engaged in the same business as its Lord: that of opening the world to its horizon, to its destiny as God's Kingdom."[3] This means that it is essentially missionary in its nature, seeking to transform the human world by communicating to it in word and act a truthfulness that exposes the deepest human fears and evasions and makes possible the kind of human existence that can pass beyond these fears to a new liberty. The Church, in claiming to exist for the sake of opening the world to the fuller life in which God can be discerned as the controlling meaning of things, claims to have something to contribute to all human cultures, all human essays in the construction of meaning. What is contributed is not easily summed up; but it is at least a Christian participation in the whole business of constructing meanings, the business of art and politics in the widest senses of those words, and at most the invitation to a new self-identification, a new self-description, in the categories of Christian prayer and sacrament. Ideally, the Christian sharing in the enterprise of art or politics is working towards the point where these new self-descriptions can be seen as possible and intelligible.

As already intimated, this work involves a passing of judgment; and here we encounter some serious difficulties. In the classical Christian story as presented in John's gospel, judgment is not effected by uttering words of condemnation but by a quite complex process of interaction. The works and words of Jesus demand choice for or against him; they force to the light hidden directions and dispositions that would otherwise never come to view, and thus make the conflicts of goals and interests between people a *public* affair. The inner rejection of one's own identity as God's creature and the object of God's love, the violence done to human truth *within* the self, becomes visible and utterable in the form of complicity in rejecting Jesus.[4] The inner readiness to come to judgment and to recognize the possibility of truth and meaning becomes visible and utterable in the form of discipleship, abiding in the community created by God's love. The dramatic event of Jesus' interaction with his people—set out in a series of ritual, quasi-legal disputations—is an event of judgment in that it gives the persons involved definitions, roles to adopt, points on

which to stand and speak.[5] They are invited to "create" themselves in finding a place within this drama—an improvisation in
the theater workshop, but one that purports to be about a comprehensive truth affecting one's identity and future. As John hints
(for instance in chapter 3), and as Paul more vividly and clearly
sees (as in Romans 11), this is far more than a simple separation
of the already godly from the already damned: the scope of Jesus'
work is the *world*—so, we must assume, the declaration of a
newly discovered identity in encounter with Jesus represents a
change for at least some. You may recognize your complicity in
the rejection of Jesus and at the same time accept the possibility
of a different role offered by the continuing merciful presence of
God in the post-Easter Jesus. In Paul's terms, all may find themselves both prisoners of disobedience and recipients of grace
(Romans 11:32).

The Gospel, then, is what enables this dual self-discovery in
women and men; and as Matthew 25 suggests, it may prove
difficult to give any general account of what a converting event
may be, because neither the rejection of Jesus nor the receiving
of his grace may readily be identifiable as such. Proclaiming the
Gospel may have much to do with the struggle to make explicit
what is at stake in particular human decisions or policies, individual and collective, and in this sense bring in the event of judgment, the revaluation of identities. I think this is rather different
from what Professor Lindbeck suggests is the goal of Christian
theology—"to discern those possibilities in current situations that
can and should be cultivated as anticipations or preparations for
the hoped for future, the coming kingdom."[6] I am wholly in
sympathy with his challenges to the "liberal" assumption that this
is to be achieved by adjusting theology to current fashion, and
what I have already said accords in important respects with his

call for discernment on the basis of criteria drawn from the specifically Christian narrative ("an intratextually derived eschatology").[7] But I want, in contrast, to argue that such discernment is not easily intelligible when divorced from the language of a transformative judgment, enacted in particular *events,* that is the central theme of so many of our foundational texts. In short, I don't think that Christian and theological discernment can ever be wholly "contemplative" and "noninterventionist"; I believe it is more importantly exercised in the discernment of what contemporary conflicts are actually *about* and in the effort both to clarify this and to decide where the Christian should find his or her identity in a conflict. The Christian is involved in seeking conversion—the bringing to judgment of contemporary struggles, and the appropriation of some new dimension of the transforming summons of Christ in his or her own life.

Here we come up against the most central issue in the whole of this discussion. How are we to speak of judgment in a fragmented culture? The language of judgment presupposes recognition and communication, the possibility of shared points of reference. To pass judgment is to propose and in certain circumstances (the law court) to effect a definitive "placing" of who or what it is that is being judged: it affects attitudes towards the object of judgment, it influences the decisions and priorities of others, it shapes what can be "claimed" by or for the object. All this applies equally to legal, artistic, and moral judgment: none of these makes sense as anything other than a public affair. To put it at its weakest: what would be *meant* by saying, "I think (judge) that the *St. Matthew Passion* is the greatest achievement of European music, but I don't care whether it's ever performed again"? Judgments take for granted a real or possible community of speaking and responding persons, and a history of concrete decisions and acts.

Hence, in a radically pluralist society, the society as such increasingly withdraws from judgment. It will contain groups who continue to believe that judgment is possible or imperative, but the social system overall sees its job as securing a pragmatic minimum of peaceful coexistence between groups, by a variety of managerial skills and economic adjustments. "Late capitalist societies are neither coherent nor integrated around a system of common values,"[8] according to the sociologist Bryan Turner, who goes on to argue that such coherence and stability as there is are secured by a mixture of diverse factors—the apparatus of modern administration itself, the neutralizing of genuine political dissent, the system of palliative welfare benefits, the reduction of the franchise to an almost passive formality, and the social dependency induced by the nature of economic and employment relations in a technologically advanced multinational economy.[9] Societies that are able to control their populations in such ways do not need the legitimization of "values"; they do not need myth or religion or morality. To put it in other terms, they can evade the question of why *this* social order should be respected, preserved, or defended, because they are not threatened, practically speaking, by their inability to answer it: they have sufficient resources, administratively and technically, to guarantee survival for the foreseeable future. If the price of survival is high (permanent large-scale unemployment, the erosion of public health care or state education, the creation of what has come to be called an "underclass"), it is still manageable, because the damaging results of the system have the effect of moving the disadvantaged further away from the processes of public decision making.

Societies like this (like the U.K. and the U.S.A. under their present governments) have no problem in tolerating a "chaos of personal life-styles" in practice, even where there may be varieties of public rhetoric that commend some lifestyles more than others.[10] In the context of these societies, indeed, *style* is everything: with massive commercial support, cultural options—even when their roots are in would-be dissident groupings—are developed and presented as consumer goods. Religious belief is no exception, whether this process of consumerization appears in the naked crudity of fundamentalist broadcasting or in the subtler ways in which secular media dictate the tone and the agenda of the behavior and utterances of religious leaders; and religious commitment is reduced to a private matter of style, unconnected with the nature of a person's membership in his or her society. Public life continues, whatever style we adopt. And concern with style notoriously detracts from seriousness about what is to be said (a point noted long ago by Augustine and others[11]): a recent series in the London *Guardian* [12] about postmodernism in the arts noted with anxiety the rising popularity of pastiche and pseudo-traditionalism alongside anarchic and parodic idioms, a kind of new baroque—two sides of the same coin.

There remains, of course, a nostalgia for "values," which the Church should beware of exploiting. The diffuse discontent that consumer pluralism can engender (although it largely contains and even utilizes it) yields itself readily to any program that dresses itself persuasively enough in moral rhetoric; but this is something essentially unrelated to how priorities are fixed in government (as recent British and American policies make depressingly clear). The Church misconceives its missionary task if it simply latches on to this kind of window dressing and echoes the individualistic and facile language of moral retrenchment that often accompanies a further intensification of administrative control and the attrition of participatory politics. To put it in language lately made familiar by Richard Neuhaus, there may be a "naked public square," but, before the churches rush into it, they have to ask whether the space opened up is genuinely a *public* one, or is simply the void defined by a system that can carry on perfectly well in the short term with this nakedness.[13]

My worry with Professor Lindbeck's proposal is that it might end up encouraging the continuance of this situation. In *The Nature of Doctrine,* he identifies with admirable precision the danger of reducing faith to a commodity marketed to atomistic selves in a hopelessly fragmented culture, and goes on to defend the idea that a unified future world rescued from the acids of modernity would be more likely to be fostered by "communal enclaves," concerned with socialization and mutual support rather than with "individual rights and entitlements," as opposed to religious traditions that eagerly abandon their distinctiveness in favor of a liberal syncretism.[14] This may be so; but unless these "enclaves" are also concerned quite explicitly with the problem of restoring an authentically public discourse in their cultural setting, they will simply collude with the dominant consumer pluralism and condemn themselves to be trivialized into stylistic preferences once more. The communal enclave, if it is not to be a ghetto, must make certain claims on the possibility of a global community, and act accordingly.

Naturally, this raises for many the specter of theocratic totalitarianism. But such an anxiety, though quite proper in itself, is not necessitated by these "claims on . . . a global community," for a number of reasons. First of all, theocracy assumes that there can be an end to dialogue and discovery; that believers would have the right (if they had the power) to outlaw unbelief. It assumes that there could be a situation in which believers in effect had nothing to learn, and therefore that the corporate conversion of the Church could be over and done with. Second, following from this, theocracy assumes an end to history. The powerful suggestions of Barth and von Balthasar[15] about history between the resurrection and the second coming as the gift of a time of repentance and growth are set aside; instead of God alone determining the end of the times of repentance, the Church seeks to foreclose the eschaton. Third, most obviously, theocracy reflects a misunderstanding of the hope for God's kingdom, a fusion of divine and earthly sovereignty in a way quite foreign to the language and practice of Jesus. Theocracy, the administration by Christians of a monolithic society in which all distinction between sin and crime is eroded, is neither a practical nor a theologically defensible goal.

The Christian claim, then, is bound *always* to be something evolving and acquiring definition in the conversations of history: it offers a direction for historical construction of human meaning, but it does not offer to end history. Like the humane Trotskyism of Raymond Williams, it envisages a "long revolution," at best an asymptotic approach to a condition that history is itself (by definition) incapable of realizing—a perfect communality of language and action free from the distortions imposed on understanding by the clash of group interests and the self-defense of the powerful.[16] The Christian may have no clearer a picture than anyone else of what this would look like, but can at least contribute specific perceptions of what holds back the coming of such a world, and specific possibilities of transforming acts and decisions—conversion in the broad sense already outlined, or what Dietrich Ritschl in his superb new book on *The Logic of Theology* calls the work of the "therapeutic spirit" in the creative renewal of persons and communities.[17]

Christians in general and theologians in particular are thus going to be involved as best they can in those enterprises in their culture that seek to create or recover a sense of shared discourse and common purpose in human society. This can mean various things. The most obvious is some sort of critical identification with whatever political groupings speak for a serious and humane resistance to consumer pluralism and the administered society. These days, such groupings are less likely than ever to be found within historic mainstream political parties, though there are some countries, happily, where moral imagination has not been so completely privatized. For many, it has been ecological issues, feminism, civil rights, and "peace" networks that have provided a new political language and a sense of the urgency and possibility of human unity. All of these are themselves in constant danger of being marginalized, and all have their fringes of mere style, apolitical and exclusivist posturing. The task of keeping them related to what remains of a democratic public process, to the parties that people actually vote for, is a hard and thankless one: if my suggestions are right, it may well be a major task for the informed Christian. But I have in mind also the work of those artists who have a commitment to the future of language and imagination: here too the Christian's business is engagement and solidarity, a willingness to listen and respond. The English playwright Howard Barker argues in the *Guardian* (February 10, 1986) for the necessity of a revival of tragedy, in order to break through the false collectivism of "populist" theatre (typified by the musical) and put people back in touch with the isolation of their own pain—a paradoxical move towards the *authentically* public by way of intensifying the personal. In Britain the television dramas of Alan Birdsdale and Dennis Potter have perhaps most vividly exemplified such a move. Can the Christian, in whatever way, help to nurture both the production and the reception of these statements? For many people, these are thresholds—perhaps more—of judgment, of "therapeutic transformation."[18] And, in a very different way, contemporary scientific and medical practice reflects the struggle between mechanistic, dominating, administrative patterns and a relatively new, tentative, not always very coherent concern for unity and interdependence. Here is a further field for learning and for solidarity.

The late Cornelius Ernst, O.P., in a seminally important essay on "Theological Methodology," argued that the meaning of the world in Christ could only be articulated in a continuing search for a "total human culture, the progressive discovery of a single human identity in Christ."[19] The form of this search was quite simply any and every process of human self-definition in response to mass culture, the threat of a "totalizing" society of technological manipulation and control. "There is at least a single discernible adversary." If the essence of the Church is missionary, this is precisely the search and the struggle to which the Church is committed. Professor Lindbeck suggests that those who give primacy to the question of how the Gospel is preached in a post-Christian environment "regularly become liberal foundationists," preoccupied with *translating* the Gospel into alien terms, or at least redefining it in response to secular questions.[20] I am not so sure. For one thing, as I have argued, preaching is not something extraneous to the identity and integrity of the Church; we are not allowed to sidestep the question. But equally, it is not clear that the only alternative to intensive in-house catechesis is translation into a foreign language in a way that sacrifices the distinctiveness of the Gospel. I don't see Cornelius Ernst as a "liberal foundationalist": he is, I think, suggesting not a search for *words* equivalent to our traditional terms (so that we presuppose a more neutral or abstract content), but a search for what recognizably—however imperfectly—shares in the same project that the Gospel defines. Can we so *rediscover* our own foundational story in the acts and hopes of others that we ourselves are reconverted and are also able to bring those acts and hopes in relation with Christ for their fulfillment by the recreating grace of God?

This is certainly a potentially riskier task than simple translation either into or out of traditional Christian and scriptural terms. The Christian engaged at the frontier with politics, art, or science will frequently find that he or she *will not know what to say*. There can be a real sense of loss in respect to traditional formulae—not because they are being translated, but because they are being tested: we are discovering whether there is any sense in which the other languages we are working with can be at home with our theology. I'd agree entirely, by the way, with Professor Lindbeck that a deeper catechesis in that theology and its images is indispensable, but I think it is so because of the testing it will endure in the process of "playing away from home," conversing with its potential allies. And to take an obvious political example—if the most plausible allies in a situation are people with similarly global commitments, the encounter is loaded with the possibilities of tragic conflict. If the most plausible ally in the Philippines or Chile or South Africa is a Marxist, the Christian may be tested to the uttermost (not every Christian with Marxist or socialist sympathies shares the optimism of many liberation theologians). The Christian woman actively involved in feminism will record the same kind of tension. The paradox of our situation often seems to be that the struggle for Christian integrity in preaching leads us close to those who least tolerate some aspects of that preaching.

The difficulty appears equally in the consequent need to know when to be silent, when to wait. This account of the Christian mission is not a recipe for talkative and confident activism; it requires something like a contemplative attention to the unfamiliar—a negative capability—a reluctance at least to force the language and behavior of others into Christian categories prematurely, remembering that our understanding of those categories themselves is still growing and changing. The premature and facile use of Christian interpretive categories in fact invites judgment of another kind. My title is deliberately ambiguous: the Church judges the world; but it also hears God's judgment on itself in the judgment passed upon it by the world. "The burden of proof lies on believers and the life they lead," writes Ritschl, pointing out the way in which, when transformation becomes no more than an inflated metaphor, the language of new creation is projected more and more towards the future: present conversion becomes accordingly unreal—verbal or figurative only.[21] Preaching cannot be heard.

But the judgment of the world can cut more deeply. The weightiest criticisms of Christian speech and practice amount to this: that Christian language actually fails to transform the world's meaning because it neglects or trivializes or evades aspects of the human. It is notoriously awkward about sexuality; it risks being unserious about death when it speaks too glibly and confidently about eternal life; it can disguise the abiding reality of unhealed and meaningless suffering. So it is that some of those most serious about the renewal of a moral discourse reject formal Christian commitment as something that would weaken or corrupt their imagination.[22] It may equally be that a Church failing to understand that the political realm is a place of spiritual decision, a place where souls are made and lost, forfeits the authority to use certain of its familiar concepts or images in the public arena. Bonhoeffer, in his justly famous meditation for his godson's baptism in May of 1944, speaks powerfully of this loss of authority: "Our church, which has been fighting in these years only for its self-preservation, as though that were an end in itself, is incapable of taking the word or reconciliation and redemption to mankind and the world. Our earlier words are therefore bound to lose their force and sense."[23] This is emphatically not a "liberal" observation or a demand for better translations into modish secularity, but a sober recognition that, in the world as it is, the right to be heard speaking about God must be earned. The Christian is at once possessed by an authoritative urgency to communicate the good news, and constrained by the awareness of how easily the words of proclamation become godless, powerless to transform. The urgency must often be channelled into listening and waiting, and into the expansion of the Christian imagination itself into something that can cope with the seriousness of the world. It is certainly true that, for any of this to be possible, there must be a real immersion in the Christian tradition itself, and to this extent Professor Lindbeck's program is rightly directed. But if I were devising schemes of Christian education, I should be inclined to set such immersion side by side with an exposure to political and cultural issues that might help to focus doctrinal language in a new way: only so, I believe, can a theological formation be an induction into *judgment*—hearing it as well as mediating it.

In the same meditation for his godson, Bonhoeffer makes one of his celebrated references to the need for a nonreligious language in which to proclaim the Gospel; "so to utter the word of

God that the world will be changed and renewed by it."[24] This will not be a conscious modernizing or secularizing of the terminology of dogma and liturgy; it is certainly not something that can be planned. It will be like Jesus' own language (and practice, we must assume) in that it effects the presence of God's peace with his creatures, and so, as Bonhoeffer says in a later letter (July, 1944), it exposes the actual godlessness of the world.[25] It is nonreligious in the sense that it is not primarily concerned with securing a space within the world for a particular specialist discourse. Whether or not it uses the word "God," it effects faith, conversion, hope. Bonhoeffer's paradigm (as the July letter explains) is the encounters in the gospels between Jesus and those he calls or heals: these are events in which people are concretely drawn into a share in the vulnerability of God, into a new kind of life and a new identity. They do not receive an additional item called faith; their ordinary existence is not reorganized, found wanting in specific respects and supplemented: it is transfigured as a whole.

Bonhoeffer might equally well have pointed to the parables of Jesus. These are not religious stories or expositions of a tradition, but crystalizations of how people decide for or against self-destruction, for or against newness of life, acceptance, relatedness. Repeatedly, as the kingdom of God is spoken of, Jesus simply presents a situation, a short narrative: like *this,* he says. The riddle of the parables, the fact that they are seen as hopelessly enigmatic by friends and enemies, lies in making the connection with one's own transformation—that is, encountering God in the parable, receiving that therapy of the spirit that Dietrich Ritschl writes of, becoming open in a certain way. This, of course, is why the Christian does not repeat the gospel parables in isolation. Only as the parables of *Jesus* can they be properly heard. They are part conversion. The skills for this may be, and should be, learned largely from scripture; yet—as was suggested at the beginning of this chapter—such learning must include those transformations of scriptural narrative that restore to us or open to us the depth of what the narrative deals with, even when these versions do not belong in a mainstream of exegesis. This is perhaps the place to mention the importance of contemporary feminist exegesis as an example of disturbing scriptural reading which forces on us the "conversion" of seeing how our own words and stories may carry sin or violence in their telling, even as they provide the resource for overcoming that sin and violence. The center may be localizable, but the boundaries are not clear. Theology should be equipping us for the recognition of and response to the parabolic in the world—all that resists the control of capital and administration and hints at or struggles to a true sharing of human understanding, in art, science, and politics. It should also equip us to speak and act parabolically as Christians, to construct in our imagining and our acting "texts" about conversion—not translations of doctrine into digestible forms, but effective images of a new world like the parables of Christ. Part of the power of T. S. Eliot's *Four Quartets* is its extraordinary reticence about recognizable Christian language. Also the force of the witness of the L'Arche communities is in what they are, collaborations of those we call handicapped and those we call normal, not in the theological articulation that may (and must) be given. *This* is what is involved in speaking parabolically, and it is action nourished by the theological grasp of what the life and death of Jesus are, by scripture and the wrestle with dogmatic and devotional tradition; but not confined by it. Such formation in our tradition goes with and presses us further into the disciplines of listening—to our own untheologized memories and context, the particularity of where we are, and to the efforts at meaning of the rest of the human race. Good doctrine teaches silence, watchfulness, and the expectation of the Spirit's drastic appearance in judgment, recognition, conversion, for us and for the whole world.

NOTES

1. George A. Lindbeck, *The Nature of Doctrine: Religion and Theology in a Postliberal Age* (Philadelphia: Westminster Press, 1984), 118.
2. On Abraham and Isaac, it is also worth looking at Eric Auerbach, *Mimesis. The Representation of Reality in Western Literature* (Princeton: Princeton University Press, 1953), ch. 1, especially pp. 8–11, where Auerbach suggests how this and kindred narratives help to construct the notion of character as it typically works in western culture. This again is an instance of our being returned to the scriptural text afresh by its own legacy as appropriated outside the theological community.
3. *For the Sake of the Kingdom: God's Church and the New Creation,* the report of the Inter-Anglican Theological and Doctrinal Commission Cincinnati: published for the Anglican Consultative Council by Forward Movement Publications, 1986), 23.
4. See, e.g., Sebastian Moore, *The Crucified is No Stranger* (New York: Seabury Press, 1977) as well as later works by the same author, for a fuller account of such a theological option.
5. On the trial motif in scripture generally and in the New Testament in particular, see Ulrich Simon, "The Transcendence of Law," *Theology* 73 (1970), 166–68, and Anthony Harvey, *Jesus on Trial. A Study in the Fourth Gospel* (London: SPCV, 1976). On the wider issue of self-identification or self-discovery through a dramatic process (to which I shall be returning later), see, above all, Hans Urs von Balthasar, "*Theodramatik,*" *Prolegomena* Vol. 1 (Einsiedeln: Johannes, 1973), particularly Part 2; discussed briefly in Rowan Williams, "Balthasar and Rahner," *The Analogy of Beauty,* ed. John Riches (Edinburgh: T. & T. Clark, 1986), 11–34, 26–27.
6. Lindbeck, *The Nature of Doctrine,* 125.
7. Ibid., 126.
8. Bryan Turner, *Religion and Social Theory* (London: Heinemann, 1983), 197.
9. Ibid., 197–98; cf. 240–1.

10. Ibid., 241.

11. It forms the central theme of Augustine's *de doctrina christiana,* Book 4.

12. December 1–3, 1986.

13. Turner, *Religion and Social Theory,* 246.

14. Lindbeck, *The Nature of Doctrine,* 126–27.

15. See Barth's *Church Dogmatics* II.2, and Balthasar's *Theology of History* (London/ New York: Sheed and Ward, 1963) and *A Theological Anthropology* (New York: Sheed and Ward, 1968).

16. Any echoes of Habermas's notion of the "ideal speech situation" are deliberate. On this concept, see John Thompson's excellent introduction to Habermas's thought in *Critical Hermeneutics. A Study in the Thought of Paul Ricoeur and Jürgen Habermas* (Cambridge (UK): Cambridge University Press, 1981), especially pp. 92–94.

17. Dietrich Ritschl, *The Logic of Theology* (London: SCM, 1986), 240; cf. 231, 275–77.

18. Ibid., 231.

19. Cornelius Ernst, "Theological Methodology," *Multiple Echo,* ed. Fergus Kerr and Timothy Radcliffe (London: Darton, Longman, Todd, 1979), 85.

20. Lindbeck, *The Nature of Doctrine,* 132.

21. Ritschl, *The Logic of Theology,* 237.

22. Angela Tilby (who has for some years done much to deepen the seriousness of religious broadcasting in the U.K.) writes in an essay entitled "Spirit of the Age. A reflection on ten years of theology, television, mad vicars and magazines" (*Christian,* Vol. 5 No. 3 [1980]): "I am disturbed to discover that the playwright Dennis Potter who has through this decade been intensely aware of the pain and ambiguity of our condition feels he *cannot* enter the community of formal Christian believing because he believes the jollity, the triviality and the half-truths masking suffering would deprive him of his power to write" (p. 12).

23. Dietrich Bonhoeffer, *Letters and Papers from Prison* (enlarged edition) (London: SCM, 1971), 300.

24. Ibid.

25. Ibid., 362.

Index